The Templeless Age

The Templeless Age

An Introduction to the History, Literature, and Theology of the "Exile"

JILL MIDDLEMAS

Westminster John Knox Press
LOUISVILLE • LONDON

Book design by Sharon Adams
Cover design by Jennifer K. Cox

First edition
Published by Westminster John Knox Press
Louisville, Kentucky

This book is printed on acid-free paper that meets the American National Standards Institute Z39.48 standard. ♾

PRINTED IN THE UNITED STATES OF AMERICA

07 08 09 10 11 12 13 14 15 16 — 10 9 8 7 6 5 4 3 2 1

Library of Congress Cataloging-in-Publication Data

Middlemas, Jill Anne.
   The templeless age : an introduction to the history, literature, and theology of the "exile" / Jill Middlemas. — 1st ed.
      p. cm.
   Includes bibliographical references and index.
   ISBN 978-0-664-23130-9 (alk. paper)
   1. Judaism—History—Post-exilic period, 586 B.C.-210 A.D.   2. Jews—History—586 B.C.-70 A.D.   3. Bible. O.T.—Criticism, interpretation, etc.   I. Title.
   BM176.M525 2007
   296.09'014—dc22   2007003695

Contents

Abbreviations

AB	Anchor Bible
ANE	the Ancient Near East
ANET	*Ancient Near Eastern Texts Relating to the Old Testament.* Edited by J. B. Pritchard. 3rd ed. Princeton, 1969.
BA	*Biblical Archaeologist*
BAR	*Biblical Archaeology Review*
BDB	Brown, F., S. R. Driver, and C. A. Briggs. *A Hebrew and English Lexicon of the Old Testament.* Oxford, 1907.
BIS	Biblical Interpretation Series
BJS	Biblical and Judaic Studies
BibOr	Biblica et orientalia
BRev	*Bible Review*
BS	Biblical Seminar
BZAW	Beihefte zur Zeitschrift für die alttestamentliche Wissenschaft
ConBOT	Coniectanea biblica: Old Testament Series
CBQ	*Catholic Biblical Quarterly*
COP	Cambridge Oriental Publications
COS	*The Context of Scipture.* Edited by W. W. Hallo (3 vols; Leiden: Brill, 1997–2002).
DMOA	Documenta et monumenta orientis antiqua
DtrH	the Deuteronomistic History
ErIsr	*Eretz-Israel*
ESHM	European Seminar in Historical Methodology
ET	English Translation

FAT	Forschungen zum Alten Testament
FIOTL	Formation and Interpretation of Old Testament Literature
FRLANT	Forschungen zur Religion und Literatur des Alten und Neuen Testaments
HeyJ	*Heythrop Journal*
HSM	Harvard Semitic Monographs
HTR	*Harvard Theological Review*
HUCA	*Hebrew Union College Annual*
IEJ	*Israel Exploration Journal*
Int	*Interpretation*
ISK	Instituttet for Sammenlignende kulturforskning
JBL	*Journal of Biblical Literature*
JJS	*Journal of Jewish Studies*
JNES	*Journal of Near Eastern Studies*
JSJSup	Journal for the Study of Judaism Supplements
JSOT	*Journal for the Study of the Old Testament*
JSOTSup	Journal for the Study of the Old Testament: Supplement Series
JSSM	Journal of Semitic Studies Monograph
JTS	*Journal of Theological Studies*
NCB	New Century Biblical Commentary
OBO	Orbis biblicus et orientalis
OBT	Overtures to Biblical Theology
OTG	Old Testament Guides
OTL	Old Testament Library
OtSt	*Oudtestamentische Studiën*
SBLDS	Society of Biblical Literature Dissertation Series
SBLMS	Society of Biblical Literature Monograph Series
SBLSymS	Society of Biblical Literature Symposium Series
SBTS	Sources for Biblical and Theological Study
SO	Symbolae osloenses
SSN	Studia semitica neerlandica
VTSup	Supplements to Vetus Testamentum
TCS	Texts from Cuneiform Sources
UF	*Ugarit-Forschungen*
VT	*Vetus Testamentum*
WBC	Word Biblical Commentary
WMANT	Wissenschaftliche Monographien zum Alten und Neuen Testament
ZAW	*Zeitschrift für die alttestamentliche Wissenschaft*

Preface

The purpose of this book is twofold. In the first place, it provides an up-to-date introduction to historical, literary, and theological insights on an important period in the history of ancient Israel. In the second place, it takes seriously concerns raised about the designation of the period following the collapse of Jerusalem in 587 BCE as the "exile." "Templeless" has been chosen, not because it rolls easily off the tongue, but because it captures a sense of the time itself, the communities that experienced the downfall of Judah, and the commonality of literature at the close of the sixth century BCE with previous literary thought and expression. Moreover, "templeless" points to the period between the two temples and thus designates a definite time frame (587–515 BCE).

The Templeless Age contains an introduction to a discussion of this period and a conclusion that points to how a redesignation might enable a different understanding of the time. The chapters between begin appropriately with a historical discussion of current thinking about the downfall of Judah in the sixth century BCE and the communities in Judah, Egypt, and Babylonia that survived the disaster. Then, five chapters introduce the thought of the period. In this new study of the literature, the material is grouped under thematic headings according to the type of reaction that seems to be reflected. The literature of the templeless age includes immediate reactions, rationalization, and the recognition of the restoration of divine commitment and care. By drawing lines of commonality between texts, this overview provides new insight into human responses to suffering and crisis. In addition, it contains brief introductions to the types of literature that stemmed from the sixth century BCE—laments, historiography, prophecy, and law.

The book is designed to highlight many of the key issues that impact the interpretation of texts and to suggest how the literature functioned in its time. Each chapter concludes with reading lists of works that are cited in the chapter or provide further reading on certain points. *The Templeless Age* is designed to be one resource for the student and scholar. Ideally, it will be used alongside other interpretations of the period and its literature. The reading lists provide access to important discussions elsewhere. They are not exhaustive, because the overall aim is to inspire further thinking and to indicate possible avenues to explore.

The book in its final form stems from a series of lectures I gave on "The Exilic Age" for the Theology Faculty at Oxford University. The lectures took into account my doctoral work on templeless Judah. In the series, held over three years, I noted points of contact between different types of biblical literature and became cognizant of how the literature itself reflects different responses to disaster. This contribution to the study of the creative and generative period of the sixth century BCE is dedicated to Professor Emeritus James D. Newsome, who inspired my interest in this period and its literature a decade ago. It is my hope that it provides a fitting tribute to his brilliance as a teacher. One of the highest compliments that has been given to academics in the UK is certainly applicable to Jim—"He is a gentleman and a scholar." By dedicating this book to Jim Newsome, I pass a torch to new students of the Bible and hope to spark challenging and inspiring thoughts in another generation.

Jill Middlemas
Oxford University, January 2007

Introduction

Between 600 and 500 BCE Israelite history is characterized by a series of dramatic changes. In general terms, these changes can be thought of as disaster, exile, and return. Traditionally labelled "the exile," this period is regarded by biblical scholars as a creative epoch in which traditions were adapted and reformulated to meet the challenges posed by political, religious, and social disruption. Significantly, it is thought to be the backdrop against which much of the interpretation and even canonization of Scripture took place.

The first part of this introduction explicates the importance of "the exile" in the Bible and critical scholarship. In particular, questions that relate to its relevance will be answered. Because certain problems appear when we discuss this time period as "the exile," the next section delineates concerns about conventional terminology and argues for reclassifying it as "the templeless age" and adjusting the dates accordingly. A brief overview of theological responses typical of the ancient world concludes the introduction.

"THE EXILE"

The exile or exilic period is conventionally defined as the time between the fall of two great cities—Jerusalem in 587 and Babylon in 539 BCE. In the beginning of the sixth century BCE Judah lost what remained of its independence through the sack of Jerusalem by the Babylonians. The fall of Jerusalem marks the final event in a long period of instability that shook the southern kingdom of Judah from the close of the seventh century

BCE. As well as destroying Jerusalem and its temple, the Babylonians deported the political, religious, and social leadership of Judah to Babylonia. In 539 BCE Cyrus, the king of Persia, assumed leadership of the Babylonian Empire by the defeat of its capital city. Sometime after that date, a number of the descendants of the deportees resettled in Jerusalem and its environs. The repatriation of the exiles is considered to have begun a period of restoration often called the postexilic period. Return to the homeland led to rebuilding the sanctuary in Jerusalem and the renewal of regular ritual in honor of the deity of ancient Israel, Yahweh.

After the exilic period, the system of governance, religion, and social institutions in what became a province of the Persian Empire named Yehud were altered to such a degree that historians and biblical scholars conceive of the exile as a decisive break or watershed. On the political front, never again would Judah be ruled by a Davidic king, and never again would Judah be a state independent of foreign control (except for a brief period under the Maccabees in the second century BCE). After the return from exile, the leadership of Yehud fell to the priesthood and to Persian-appointed governors. Religiously, the temple cult after the exilic age looked very different in terms of leadership, operation, and regulation. Before the fall of Jerusalem, the religion in Judah can be characterized as Yahwistic. Although a variety of forms of the worship of Yahweh existed, the form beginning to dominate at that time was monotheistic, aniconic, and oriented to one central sanctuary. After the exile, Yahwistic religion can be characterized as exclusively monotheistic with a greater emphasis on individual religious expression. From the middle of the fourth century BCE onward, an early, yet recognizable, form of Judaism emerged, and prophecy shifted from large collections like Isaiah, Jeremiah, and Ezekiel to the more practical prophetic activity of Haggai and Zechariah.

It is with reference to religious development that the exile is especially studied. During this time four major ideological shifts were made in the religious thought of ancient Israel—two concerning conceptions of the deity and two concerning an understanding of human response. With regard to conceptions of the deity, the first major shift is the growth of monotheism. Before the exile there was a tendency to worship Yahweh in preference to other deities; this is monolatry rather than monotheism (Lang 1983). The prophetic literature represents a shift in emphasis toward the worship of Yahweh alone. This ideology is sometimes thought of as the "Yahweh alone" movement (M. Smith 1987). In the postexilic period, Yahweh was worshiped in a form of monotheism that denied even the existence of other deities.

The second major theological shift is the development of an understanding of Yahweh's rule as universal, such that the deity came to be understood as the sovereign of all the earth, with purposes for the nations, rather than just for the covenant people of ancient Israel. In the literature of the time, the governance of Yahweh included purposes for peoples not only from the land of Judah. Correspondingly, the community in Yehud struggled with questions relating to the inclusion of foreign nations and peoples within the divine purposes for humankind.

In response to this altered understanding of Yahweh and his sovereignty, greater significance was ascribed to the role of the human being. First, there is a noticeable shift to personal piety and confessional activity. Before the collapse of Judah, Yahweh was worshiped in a variety of ways and in a variety of places, even after the centralization of the cult in the Jerusalem temple. Afterwards, religious belief concentrated on clear guidelines and regulations for worship. These represent an early form of Judaism. Julius Wellhausen is the name most commonly associated with the recognition of the shift from Yahwism to Judaism brought about by the exile (Wellhausen 1885, ET 1957; Knight 1983; Barton 1995).

Secondly, in conjunction with the increased significance of human response, the exilic period is often thought to be the time during which the belief in individual responsibility arose. Guilt was no longer understood to pass from generation to generation; each person's behavior was thought to determine his or her own fate.

TERMINOLOGY AND DATING: WHY THE TEMPLELESS AGE?

Although its significance is rarely questioned, the use of exile or exilic age to denote the time between 587 and 539 has raised several important concerns. There are five chief problems with the current and traditional terminology for this period.

1. The most obvious difficulty has to do with the use of the term in the singular. According to the biblical record, the Babylonians deported people from the homeland of Judah in three separate instances in 598, 587, and 582. The term "exile" implies that there was a single deportation of citizenry from the homeland, when there were in fact several instances of forced relocation.
2. "Exile" does not adequately represent the fact that some people chose to flee from Judah. After 587 groups reportedly settled in the neighboring nation-states of Ammon, Moab, and Edom,

and, following the assassination of Gedaliah, another group fled to Egypt. For these voluntary refugees the identification of the period would be labeled more suitably the "expatriate" or the "refugee" period.

3. More importantly, the use of the term "exile" raises further concerns about the perspective of modern critical scholarship. In a descriptive and conceptual sense, exile or exilic is a misnomer. The period can be spoken of as exilic only when the perspective taken is that of the community that experienced forced relocation outside the land of Judah (Carroll 1992; Grabbe 1998). An exile exists only from the point of view of people who have been deported. The people who remained in Judah did not regard the forced relocation of some citizens in any special way. In their view, the exile was just one consequence of a wider disaster. Naturally, they never used this term for their own situation. However, the population deported to Babylonia spoke of itself as the *golah*—that is, the community taken into exile. The term "exile," then, fails to account for the variety of communities—including those who remained in Judah and those who fled to neighboring city-states—that experienced the catastrophic collapse of Judah in the early sixth century BCE. Moreover, it fails to capture the wide varieties of disaster that struck the nation. In addition to exile, the people were subject to a lengthy siege and military engagement that led to injury, death, starvation, sickness, and sexual abuse.

4. Much scholarly reference to the exile adopts uncritically the perspective of the community transferred to Babylon, which viewed its return as the fulfillment of prophecies of restoration and itself as the righteous remnant. Around this conception arose a spurious portrait, sometimes called the "myth of the empty land," that quite effectively blotted out the experience of those who remained in the land of Judah after 587 (Carroll 1992; Barstad 1996; Grabbe 1998). In later literature—Chronicles, for instance—the land of Judah is spoken of as if it had been emptied of its inhabitants. For the Chronicler it was necessary for the land to experience a Sabbath rest in order to be purified of idolatry (2 Chr. 36:21; cf. Lev. 26:34, 35, 43). To speak of the period following the destruction of Jerusalem as the exile implicitly adopts a later, not entirely accurate biblical representation in which the land lay fallow awaiting the renewal

and restoration brought about through the repatriation of those forcibly deported. Although the literature of the time conceives of an empty Judah—"So Judah went into exile out of its land" (2 Kgs. 25:21)—it also clearly acknowledges the continued habitation of the poorest people, who were left to tend to the soil (2 Kgs. 25:8–12; Jer. 52:12–16). In order to avoid either misrepresenting the period itself or the uncritical adoption of an ideological portrait from a later period, it is wise to be cautious about the use of the terms exile and exilic.

5. Finally, the notion that the exile connotes a period of time raises separate questions about conceptions of these historical events. In discussions of the exilic age an automatic assumption is that it represents a designated time frame with a clear beginning and ending. In fact, the exile in certain respects never ceased. Although descendants of the deportees traveled back to the homeland, not all dispersed Judahites chose to return. In fact, the situation of the exile par excellence never actually ceased to exist. Communities continued to live and prosper in Egypt and Babylon well beyond 539 and even represent some of the foundational and significant contributors to the continuation of Israelite religion. The Egyptian community provided the Septuagint translation of the Hebrew Bible into Greek whilst their compatriots in Babylon were responsible for the Babylonian Talmud in the rabbinic period. Moreover, from its inception Jewish history can be viewed as a series of exiles and restorations.

Taking into account these objections to the use of the term exile, there is a term that would be more appropriate to the situation: "templeless." What has heretofore been known as the exile should be viewed from the perspective of the time when each community, whether in the homeland or in voluntary or involuntary diaspora, had to deal with the loss of the Jerusalem temple. However we understand the significance of the temple, it cannot be denied that it represented the central sanctuary of the kingdom of Judah in the preexilic (or the First Temple) period and that of the province Yehud in the postexilic (or the Second Temple) period. Its loss was keenly felt during the sixth century BCE, and its restoration remained a significant feature of the prophecies about the future renewal of Jerusalem. If this understanding of the time were to be adopted, the templeless age would extend from 587 (the destruction of the temple) to 515 (when the temple was rebuilt in Jerusalem, according to the biblical account). If we define the period thus, we find that the events surrounding the destruction of the city of Jerusalem and the central sanctuary establish a definable chronological period—that is, the time between the two temples—as well as remaining consistent with theological reflection in which the lack of the sanctuary as a symbol of Yahweh's abiding presence formed a significant motif.

The templeless age (587–515) thus presents us with a clearly defined period of time in which the lack of a temple provided the backdrop against which creative contributions to the history and religion of ancient Israel were made.

This realignment in our terminology and conceptualization actually facilitates a more helpful assessment of the history and literature of the time. Exile implies an event and suggests nothing further about the period or about what type of literature was generated. The use of "templeless" to define this age more accurately invites an understanding of the diversity it entailed, not only historically from the perspective of three communities in different locations—the *golah*, the inhabitants in the homeland, and the refugees—but also literarily, from the perspective of loss and of restoration. Additionally, it takes account of recent studies that have drawn attention to the great affinity between the material culture and literary thought of the exilic period and the early postexilic period, that is, that time around the reconstruction of the temple associated with the prophets Haggai and Zechariah.

THEOLOGICAL RESPONSE TO DISASTER AND DEFEAT

The fall of Jerusalem created an unprecedented situation in which the symbolic universe of the kingdom of Judah was drastically called into question. The Babylonians destroyed two foundational symbols of Yahweh's presence and protection—the king and temple. A symbolic collapse of this magnitude necessitated some type of response. In the literature of this period, the catastrophe influenced conceptions of the deity and religiosity. Because people in the ancient world conceived of everyday existence and monumental events as having much to do with the divine realm, disasters—natural or otherwise—resulted in intensive theological reflection. Throughout the ancient world, the destruction of a city, defeat in battle, and the ruination of a temple resulted in reformulations of divine volition and intention or even neglect. (As we shall see, biblical writers of the time conceived of the fall of Jerusalem as either the result of Yahweh's anger and judgment or as a consequence of his withdrawal of support.)

In response to such political, religious, and social disasters, people of the ancient world not only reformulated their conceptions of deity; they also reconfigured their understanding of religious identity and expression. Bob Becking suggests four possible changes in religious thought common to ancient societies reacting to defeat (1999; cf. Ackroyd 1994: 39–49):

1. The abandonment of traditional religion in favor of the foreign conquering religion.
2. Continuity with or reinforcement of indigenous elements in religion. (In terms of Yahwistic religion, this would coincide with the resurgence of worship practices thought to be Canaanite or foreign in origin.)
3. Concentration on religion as orthodox and monotheistic.
4. The reformulation of religion in a new political and social context.

The Hebrew Bible survives today and remains a foundational document for religious identity because creative and innovative thinkers were able to assess the catastrophic events that transpired in and after 587 within a theological framework that allowed for the reevaluation and re-presentation of traditions. Historians, priests, and prophets conceived of new ideas in the face of harsh reality and suffering that helped to maintain the religion and society of a people who experienced the loss of their nation. In the literature of the templeless age and beyond, there is evidence of all four religious reactions listed above.

OVERVIEW

This book provides an introduction to the history and literature of the creative and generative templeless age. Chapter 1 covers the historical events surrounding the final fall of Jerusalem in 587 BCE. In addition, it surveys current assessments of the experience of the communities that continued to exist during the period in their three very different social settings: in the homeland of Judah, in the Diaspora in Babylon, and in the Diaspora in Egypt. Subsequent chapters provide an introduction to the religious literature associated with the time, categorized along thematic lines rather than according to biblical books.

Three main categories are distinguished:

1. Chapters 2 and 3 deal with literature lacking a future vision, as expressed in two genres: lamentation (certain psalms, Isa.

63:7–64:11, and Lamentations) and historiography (the Deuteronomistic History).

2. Chapter 4 considers literature characterized by the intermingling of judgment and hope (Jeremiah and Ezekiel).

3. Chapters 5 and 6 cover literature exemplifing a turn to hope: hope in divine reversal (Deutero-Isaiah and Ezek. 40–48), and hope in faithful human response to divine salvation (Haggai, Zech. 1–8, and the Holiness Code).

CHAPTER 1

The Historical Record

This first chapter begins with a brief discussion of some of the problems in assessing the historical portrait of the period under Babylonian rule, but concludes that the Hebrew Bible may profitably be used as a source of information. The comments are followed by a reconstruction of the period based on historical, archaeological, and imperial data as well as an overview of the situation of the communities that survived the collapse of Judah.

The use of the Hebrew Bible as a source of historical information has come under increased scrutiny in recent years. Serious studies have challenged the biblical perspective as ideologically rather than factually based (Edelman 1991; Davies 1995; Grabbe 1998; Long 1999). In addition, there is a gap in the presentation of biblical historiography. The account in 2 Kings ends at the point of devastation (2 Kgs. 25), and the biblical story resumes with the events surrounding the reconstruction of the temple towards the end of the sixth century BCE in Ezra 1–6. Because of increased concerns about the use of the Bible in historical reconstructions, appeals have been made to archaeological evidence and imperial ruling strategies. The archaeological evidence and imperial ruling policies yield a relatively skeletal portrait of sixth-century Judah, however. Moreover, neither provides complete and incontrovertible details for the period under question. Through archaeological excavations, the material culture reveals details of only a general nature, such as the locations of cities and regions with destruction layers and areas of continued habitation. A consideration of the ruling strategies of the Neo-Babylonians adds only minimally to this portrait, as there are no cuneiform records dealing with Neo-Babylonian rule in Judah. Scholars have suggested that Judah became a province in the Babylonian Empire by appeal to hints in the biblical narrative (Lipschits 1998; 2005) and analogies to Babylonian policies elsewhere (Middlemas 2005:48–70). Even if the status of Judah could be ascertained with certainty, it remains unclear how Neo-Babylonian rule affected the western periphery.

On the basis of archaeological and imperial evidence alone, the historian is left with crucial questions unanswered: Who were the people devastated by attack in the sixth century BCE? What was their perspective on the widespread devastation? An examination of ancient Israel simply cannot be undertaken without the use of the biblical witness. The narrative that follows seeks to answer some of these questions using biblical and ancient Near Eastern (ANE) references where applicable. Nevertheless, cautions about the use of the Bible deserve attention because the purpose of the Hebrew Bible is not to record history, but to preserve an interpretation of events from the perspective of the interaction of a people and their god. The biblical details are included in the portrait of the period that follows, not because they depict events exactly as they transpired in sixth-century Judah, because texts are not windows into history (Barstad 1998). They appear because they alone provide details about a people and a place with which we are concerned (Miller 1991). History in the biblical documents provides information about the way the biblical writers conceived of and understood their past.

OVERVIEW OF THE TEMPLELESS AGE (587–515 BCE)

Toward the end of the seventh century BCE the Assyrian hold over its empire—stretching from the Zagros foothills to the border of Egypt— began to wane. The Neo-Babylonians under the leadership of Nabopolassar gained control of the Assyrian Empire by taking its capital city, Nineveh, in 612 BCE (recorded in the Gadd Chronicle, currently housed in the British Museum). In conjunction with its collapse, the lands of the empire remained in a state of flux during which Babylon (the new kingdom established in the seventh century BCE, generally referred to as that of the Neo-Babylonians) and Egypt vied for control over the Levant, including the Transjordan region. The son of Nabopolassar, Nebuchadnezzar, gained total control of the former Assyrian Empire through the decisive defeat of the Egyptian army at Carchemish in 605. Caught in the middle of a power struggle between Egypt and Babylon, Judah, during the rule of King Jehoiakim, aligned itself with Egypt and in 601 rebelled against Babylonian vassalage to its detriment. Since treaties outlined a series of escalating punishments for infractions, Nebuchadnezzar responded with an incursion against Jerusalem in 598. In the intervening few years, Jehoiakim had died and his young son, Jehoiachin, had ascended the throne (2 Kgs. 24:8). A change in leadership notwithstanding, in 598 the Neo-Babylonian troops besieged, captured, and looted Jerusalem, and exiled the king and members of the royal household, leading citizens, and artisans to Babylon (2 Kgs. 24:10–17). The Neo-Babylonians replaced the deposed King Jehoiachin with his uncle, Mattaniah-Zedekiah. An account in a series of royal annals that recorded the activities of the Babylonian kings termed the Babylonian Chronicles confirms the rough details of the biblical account:

> The seventh year, in the month of Kislev, the king of Akkad mustered his troops, marched on Hatti, and set up his quarters facing the city of Yehud. In the month of Adar, the second day, he took the city and captured the king. He installed there a king of his choice. He colle[cted] its massive tribute and went back to Babylon.[1]

Zedekiah was the last of the kings of Judah. Against the advice of the vociferous Jeremiah, in 588 he rebelled against Babylon, in what was to be the final attempt at gaining independence. The Neo-Babylonians responded swiftly to the treaty infraction with an attack on Jerusalem and its environs that eradicated the meaningful political, social, and religious symbols of Judah. In either the eighteenth (Jer. 52:29) or the nineteenth (2 Kgs. 25:8) year of the reign of Nebuchadnezzar, the city of Jerusalem was besieged, captured, sacked, looted, and razed, and those inhabitants who did not fall in battle were deported to Babylon, with only the very "poorest people of the land [left] to be vinedressers and tillers of the soil" (2 Kgs. 25:8–12; Jer. 39:8–10; 52:12–16). Thus "Judah went into exile out of its land" (2 Kgs. 25:21; Jer. 52:27). King Zedekiah was forced to watch the murder of his sons before being blinded and taken in chains to Babylonia (2 Kgs. 25:6–7// Jer. 39:5–7; 52:9–11). Besides being a punitive response, the second Babylonian attack on Jerusalem was designed to contribute to a decisive policy in the region in order to generate stability. Before its attack on Jerusalem, the Neo-Babylonians had almost completely eradicated the Philistine cities of Ashkelon and Ashdod as a means

---

1. Glassner 2004: 231. Regrettably, the Babylonian Chronicles break off after the eleventh year of Nebuchadnezzar (594), to be resumed only some thirty years later.

to create a buffer zone between the empire and troublesome Egypt (Stager 1996a; 1996b).

Although Judah was severely crippled, the Neo-Babylonians reinstated a degree of stability by installing Gedaliah as governor in Mizpah (roughly nineteen miles north of Jerusalem) over the newly established imperial province (2 Kgs. 25:22–26; Jer. 40:7–41:15). Those who had hidden among caves and in the rough terrain surrounding Jerusalem came to Mizpah (2 Kgs. 25:23; Jer. 40:7), along with others who had fled to various Transjordanian kingdoms (Jer. 40:11–12). Measures taken to promote stability and regeneration were cut short when a group of royalists assassinated Gedaliah (2 Kgs. 25:25; Jer. 41:1–2, 18). Fearing Babylonian response, the insurgents fled to Egypt, reputedly with Jeremiah in tow. A further deportation in 582 may be linked to an imperial response to the assassination of the Babylonian appointee, Gedaliah (Jer. 52:30). Information about the population in the land ceases at this point. In fact, the books of Kings and Jeremiah end with an aside about King Jehoiachin in Babylon released from prison in 562 (2 Kgs. 25:27–30//Jer. 52:31–34). Cuneiform texts commonly known as the Weidner documents account for the daily allowance of food and drink allotted to Jehoiachin and members of his family in Babylon (*ANET* 308).

After the death of Nebuchadnezzar in 561, the Neo-Babylonian Empire entered a period of sharp decline. A quick succession of three kings finally resulted in the rise to power of the mature Nabonidus (555–539). In 550 BCE a new wind began to blow in the ancient Near East. In that year, Cyrus rallied the tribes of Persia and conquered the neighboring Median kingdom. This marked the beginning of the rise to power of the Persians. According to the Nabonidus Chronicle, in 539 Cyrus entered Babylon accompanied by much fanfare and took it without bloodshed (Babylonian Chronicle 7 iii 12–16, 18). The end of the exile is usually dated to the overthrow of Babylon in 539. The following year, in 538, Cyrus issued an edict, recorded on what is known as the Cyrus Cylinder (housed in the British Museum), ordering the return of cult statues and deported peoples to various places around Babylon (*COS* 3: 314–16). Although Old Testament scholars have greeted what is known as the Cyrus Cylinder with exuberant, almost wild, speculation about the enlightened, liberal, and humane attitude of Cyrus towards subject peoples, difficulties have been raised with interpreting it as an empirewide policy, as it concerned only Babylonian cultic sites (Kuhrt 1983; Bedford 2001). A Cyrus edict issued for the restoration of the cult in Jerusalem, however, is found in the Hebrew Bible in a Hebrew version in Ezra 1:2–4 and in Aramaic in Ezra 6:2–5. The biblical versions proclaim Yahweh's choice of Cyrus as a means to liberate the exiles in Babylon and restore the Jerusalem temple. The authenticity of a specific declaration to the Jews allowing them to return to Judah is questionable (see Bedford 2001 for a recent analysis of the discussion). At the very least, the Cyrus Cylinder suggests that the Persians would not have interfered with the reconstruction of the temple in Jerusalem.

What has traditionally been referred to as the early postexilic period, 539–515 BCE, actually forms a natural conclusion to the templeless age. The material culture and ethos of these twenty-five years share more with the preceding period than with the following years. During this time, the Persian kings, mainly Cyrus and Cambyses, set about to consolidate and stabilize the empire through military campaigns. Cyrus died in one such campaign and was succeeded in 527 by his son Cambyses, whose greatest military achievement was the subjugation of Egypt in 525. After his death under mysterious circumstances in 522, the empire was rocked by a series of rebellions during which various pretenders vied for the throne. During this precarious time, Darius, distantly related to the line of Cyrus, assumed the leadership. He spent the next few years quashing countries that had utilized the disarray within the empire to assert independence. A brilliant strategist, Darius maintained control of the greatest empire ever seen in the ancient Near East at that time by instigating sweeping reforms. Along with connecting the distant reaches of the empire by improved highway and messenger systems, he sought the favor of subject peoples diplomatically by utilizing the talents of local leaders in government and providing the opportunity and means to rebuild temples that had lain in ruin from the time of the Babylonians.

Presumably, there were waves of exiles who returned to Judah during this time, although the events themselves inspired no literary record contemporaneous with the events themselves (but see Ezra 1–6 for a reconstruction of the events from a later time). Archaeological evidence shows an interesting phenomenon in settlement patterns at the end of the sixth century. Sites in the Benjamin region to the north of Jerusalem decrease or cease to exist altogether, and new sites spring up in the south in and around Jerusalem. It has been argued that the shift in population may reflect a Persian policy of repatriation (Hoglund 1991; 1992), but the conditions under which the movement occurred suggest economic and agricultural reasons (Lipschits 1999: 182–85). Judah itself was marked by a depressed economy and agricultural difficulties brought on by drought. Under the prophetic authority of Haggai and Zechariah (chaps.

1–8) and the leadership of Sheshbazzar and Zerubbabel, the temple was rebuilt in Jerusalem (Ezra 1–6). Its dedication in 515 BCE (Ezra 6:15) marks the close of the templeless age.

The character of the community at the close of the sixth century BCE remains open to dispute. Two recent assessments of the sources of events that transpired around the reconstruction of the temple deserve mention here. The first is a careful and well-researched examination of the pertinent biblical material by Peter Bedford (2001). In his study of the social context in which the rebuilding of the temple took place, he reassesses biblical and ancient Near Eastern evidence in the light of the reconstructions of interpreters. He has shown that the social situation of a later time (that portrayed in Ezra 1–6) has been read back into the sources of the period. Resisting the temptation to adopt the ideological perspective of the fifth century allows for an analysis of the late-sixth-century prophets (Haggai and Zechariah 1–8, along with Ezra 5–6) that reveals an integrated community drawing on its past traditions to reformulate its identity as Yahweh's people.

In contrast to Bedford, Lipschits represents the standard view in that he has adopted the portrait of Ezra 1–6 in his reconstruction of late-sixth-century Judah and asserted the existence of a societal rift (Lipschits 2005: 358–59). In this view, a division was created by conflict between the nonrepatriated community, which had assumed positions of leadership as well as possession of the land, and the repatriated exiles, who struggled for the return of power and property. However, Bedford's analyses have shown that the language of Haggai and Zechariah was not exclusive and that temple rebuilding created the opportunity for social integration. Furthermore, Hoffman, in his studies of references to the fasts in Zechariah 7 (2003) shows that the prophet mentions fast days observed by the community in the homeland and the *golah* as a way of linking the interests of the society. Early attempts were made to forge a unified identity.

Lipschits bases his interpretation in part on the addition of polemical appendices to the Deuteronomistic History after the return to Zion. The provenance of the material cited, however, is more widely recognized by scholars as having stemmed from the literary activity that took place among the population in Babylon. Polemical passages in the literature of the exiles against Neo-Babylonian Judah are a well-known feature of sixth-century prophecy attributed to the exiles (Middlemas 2005: 72–121). The polemical appendices noted by Lipschits are included in exilic literature before repatriation and serve as a literary means of explaining the deity's reasons for the downfall of Judah. As such, they cannot provide evidence of an emerging division in society after the return of exiles.

Another important challenge to prevalent views about temple reconstruction has been launched by Diana Edelman. She argues that the temple was rebuilt around the time of Nehemiah, who was active in the fifth century BCE (Edelman 2005). Her argument raises doubts about the chronology found in the Hebrew Bible and advances material evidence that favors a later date. This approach, however, shows little awareness of critical work on biblical literature that would contradict the locating of certain texts in the fifth century BCE. For example, one of Edelman's arguments rests on discounting the chronological framework of Haggai and Zechariah 1–8 as a later ideological addition supplied to correlate Jeremiah's prophecy of a seventy-year exile with the completion of the sanctuary. It is true that scholars have long attributed an editorial framework to the prophecies of Haggai and Zechariah 1–8, but Ackroyd (1951; 1952) and Mason (1977; 1984) have shown that the outlook and vocabulary of this framework are similar to the words of the prophets. Although the framework is later, it is not significantly later than the prophecies themselves. Moreover, the material exhibits no point of contact with the views prevalent in Ezra and Nehemiah, who perceive a societal schism and attempt programmatically to exclude foreigners from the community. Furthermore, one of the purposes of Haggai and Zechariah is to reestablish the centrality of Jerusalem and its temple, a premise that Ezra and Nehemiah take for granted. When the editorial framework is removed, the prophecies about temple building in Haggai and Zechariah still urge building work and the centrality of Jerusalem. Because they do not share similarities with Ezra and Nehemiah, it is not possible simply to remove the dating scheme to suggest they belong to a different time. Other factors besides the ascription of a chronology influence how time is perceived. It may be that interpreters need to reassess the evidence for positing the date of the reconstructed temple in 515 BCE rather than a later time; however, for the purposes of this study, the biblical understanding of history provides a plausible time frame for the templeless age and will be upheld.

Archaeological excavations have provided evidence of new sites in and around Jerusalem at the close of the sixth century BCE, suggestive of the return of exiles and likely a number of refugees as well. Haggai and Zechariah 1–8 provide a glimpse of the community at that time. The remnant and the repatriates worked together to rebuild their identity, reorganize their society, and reconstruct the temple of their deity, Yahweh.

THE HOMELAND: LIFE IN JUDAH

Historical references to the remaining inhabitants of Judah, although sketchy, at best suggest that the aftermath of war resulted in widespread physical devastation and significant human tragedy. In terms of human suffering, the book of Lamentations explores in graphic detail the dire consequences of war for the people of Jerusalem and Judah. Besides enduring disgrace and humiliation, the people suffered from slaughter, sickness, sexual abuse, and starvation. The archaeological evidence supports to some extent the grim portrait of a devastated and crippled Judah evoked by the historical record. The southern territory around and including Jerusalem was especially hard hit. Many of the twenty-two sites in which destruction layers have been found were uninhabited during the sixth century BCE. Jerusalem itself appears to have had only minimal habitation. Loss of territory due to the encroachment from neighboring nation-states was also a problem (the Ammonites in Jer. 49:1–5; the Edomites in Jer. 49:7–22 and Obadiah) (Albertz 2003).

There are several indications that the situation in other parts of the country was not as dire as the laments or the widespread archaeological excavations attest. The sites with devastation layers are located primarily in the southern territory of Judah. It has long been recognized that the territory of Benjamin, north of Judah, survived the Babylonian campaigns virtually unscathed. More importantly, several sites show continued settlement and a return to normal existence during the sixth century BCE. One such is Mizpah (*Tell en-Nasbeh*), whose role as the administrative center of the province has received greater attention in scholarship in recent years, due partly to the work of Jeffrey Zorn (1997; 2003) and Oded Lipschits (1998; 1999; 2001; 2005). Evidence thus emerges of resurgence and renewal in the homeland, particularly in the Benjamin region.

The quality of life in the homeland remains a matter of debate. On the one hand, the archaeologist Ephraim Stern (2001; 2002) concentrates on evidence of widespread devastation and argues for subsistence-level survival in the homeland. On the other hand, Hans Barstad (1996) and Joseph Blenkinsopp (2002a and b), noting areas of settlement and even prosperity from excavations to the north of Jerusalem, argue for the return to stable community life (see also Lipschits 2005; Middlemas 2005). Unfortunately, the uncertainty surrounding Babylonian imperial policies outside of Mesopotamia, due to the lack of material evidence, does little to adjudicate between the conflicting reconstructions of life in Judah. Because their homeland had relatively few natural resources, the Mesopotamian empires long sought to extend their rule to other regions, in order to maximize the movement of goods and raw materials into the Assyrian or Babylonian heartlands. Under Tiglath-pileser III in the mid-eighth century BCE the Assyrians developed a provincial system in which governed states paid taxes usually in the form of goods—raw materials, luxury items, food stuffs, or wine. There has been some debate about whether or not the Babylonians adopted this model. The issue rests ultimately on whether they encouraged the reinstatement of normality in states of the empire (Barstad 1996) or used military force to collect tribute on a yearly basis (Vanderhooft 1999; 2003). In the former model a state would fare quite well with reasonably little interference from the imperial overlord while in the latter a state would fare poorly, by existing outside an integrated imperial system that supported trade and by having its wealth taken away via annual devastating military campaigns. The most recent studies of imperial rule during the period have suggested that, because of Neo-Babylonian concerns abotu Egypt, there was a shift in ruling strategies whereby Judah was made a province, in an effort to promote loyalty and stability (Lipschits 2005; Middlemas 2005).

Judah was known in the ancient Near East for producing certain types of luxury items that would also have been desirable goods in the markets of Babylonia. The fact that the biblical account notes that the Neo-Babylonians left "vinedressers and tillers of the soil" indicates imperial intentions to encourage trade. Not only would goods be required in Babylon, which was currently undergoing its renaissance or golden age, but the government made money from levying taxes on the movement of items across the empire. Certain biblical references suggest that the Neo-Babylonians levied heavy taxes on Judah (Lam. 5:3–6, 8–10, 13; Hag. 1:6). The initial actions of the Neo-Babylonians in Judah suggest an interest in generating a stable situation. Based on certain texts in Jeremiah, Lipschits argues that Nebuchadnezzar established Mizpah as an administrative center before the destruction of Jerusalem (2005). The archaeological excavations of the site led by Zorn support his contention in that they provide evidence of construction work consistent with the creation of an administrative center (1997; 2003). Moreover, the Babylonian king contributed to the regeneration of stability through the installation of Gedaliah as a governor or puppet-king.[2]

---

2. The biblical writers never use the term "governor" for Gedaliah, but the Hebrew term used of his rule ("to designate, set up," the *hiphil* of *paqad*) certainly implies that he functioned in this capacity. Miller and Hayes 2006: 482–85, among others, argue that he was installed as king.

It has generally been assumed that Babylonian interest in stimulating the renewal of Judah ceased after the assassination of Gedaliah (Lipschits 2005: 118–22). Nevertheless, it is likely that certain leaders of the community organized to establish an alternative authoritative figure. During the period of the monarchy when the stability of the nation was threatened by uncertainty surrounding the succession of the throne, "the people of the land" (2 Kgs. 11:13–20; 21:24; 23:30) or "the people of Judah" (2 Kgs. 14:19–22) intervened to place someone on the throne as quickly as possible (Seitz 1989). The "people of the land" are thought to have been full citizens who owned land (see Fried 2006, for a recent overview) and lived, primarily, outside of Jerusalem and therefore remained in Judah after the Babylonian incursions. After the assassination of Gedaliah, this same group would likely be responsible for reasserting stability by appointing a governor. Furthermore, Christopher Seitz has argued that a scribal class existed around Jeremiah and recorded positive prophecies toward the community in Judah before the death of Gedaliah (1989; the Shaphan family is also mentioned in Lipschits 2005). Ongoing prophetic and literary activity would suggest a degree of normality.

A growing number of scholars regard the situation in Judah to have been sufficiently stable to support general well-being and theological activity. A stable community with its own political authority would allow for the continuation of worship and literary production. The temple, if not completely torn down, was certainly desecrated (Jones 1963). In terms of the religious life of the community, the pilgrimage of a party of mourning men from Shechem, Shiloh, and Samaria bearing cereal and incense offerings to the temple site, to the house of Yahweh (*beth Yhwh*) in Jeremiah 41:5 provides some indication that cultic activity continued, albeit reduced in scale. The actions of the men, furthermore, suggest the presence of spontaneous and sporadic worship at the ruins of the sanctuary. Since ritual activity would exist alongside a normally functioning state, a sanctuary was probably established to facilitate regular worship. On the possibilities for cultic renewal outside of Jerusalem, Blenkinsopp has pointed to the possibility of a sanctuary in Bethel, long a sacred cultic site in the near vicinity of Mizpah (2002a and b); but other sites in Mizpah, Gibeah, and Gibeon may have been operative as well (Edelman 2002; Lipschits 2005). The widely agreed location of the book of Lamentations in Neo-Babylonian Judah suggests a cultic center would have been operative during the time (Middlemas 2005). Finally, it is relatively clear that although social, political, and religious life resumed in the land, it was not entirely comfortable or free from foreign interference.

THE DIASPORA: LIFE AND THOUGHT IN EGYPT AND BABYLON

In addition to disaster, the destruction of Jerusalem in 587 resulted in deportation and the dispersion of Judahites. Two main places became the locus of Diaspora communities: Egypt and Babylon. Both will be discussed in terms of historical information and the reactions to disaster that took place therein.

Egypt

Following the successful royalist attack on Gedaliah, a number of Judahites fled to Egypt for refuge. According to 2 Kings 25:26, "Then all the people, high and low, and the captains of the forces set out and went to Egypt; for they were afraid of the Chaldeans." Refugees who fled to Egypt settled in Tahpahnes in lower Egypt (Jer. 43:7) and in Migdol, Memphis, and the land of Pathros (Jer. 44:1). These place names include locations in Upper and Lower Egypt and probably serve to include Jews in the totality of Egypt.

There is very little information on the refugees who fled to Egypt to escape the wrath of Nebuchadnezzar after the assassination of Gedaliah. Sources of information include 2 Kings 25, Jeremiah 42–44, and Ezekiel 29–32, along with extrabiblical material from a colony of Jewish soldiers and their families at Elephantine (modern-day Aswan) (Porten 1968; 1996; 2003). Jeremiah condemns the refugees in Egypt for worshiping other deities, while Ezekiel includes Egypt in an oracle of doom. In addition, Aramaic documents from Elephantine dating to the fifth and fourth centuries BCE give a general sketch of Jewish life in Egypt. The Elephantine Papyri contain letters and contracts that include details about worship and civil practices. Although the origins of the Elephantine community are unknown, it is thought that their residence in Egypt is unconnected to the fall of Judah.

The Elephantine papyri are especially helpful in providing a glimpse of what life would have been like in Egypt. However, it should be born in mind that they stem from a time later than the templeless age. At the first cataract of the Nile, an island called Elephantine juts out. A Jewish garrison with their wives and children were placed here by the Egyptians to ward against any attack from states to the south. The Jewish colonies at Migdol, Tahpanhes, and Memphis named in Jeremiah 46:14 may also have been military colonies; little information has been forthcoming to clarify their origin. An addition to the book of Isaiah possibly refers to Elephantine as "a pillar to the Lord" at the border of Egypt (Isa. 19:19).

The community claims to have resided in Elephantine prior to the arrival of Cambyses in Egypt in 527 (*COS* 3: 125–30).

As with any mercenary military force, the Jewish garrison would have received payment and land grants from the Egyptian government. They went about their daily affairs with relative autonomy in judicial and religious matters. Intermarriage and religious assimilation were possible. In terms of social structure, it is clear from deeds and business documents that the status of women was elevated. They could own property, make decisions about their property, issue a divorce, read, and be named members of the community. If, as some believe, the community represents a continuation of Israelite society from before the collapse of Judah, it would suggest that the status of women diminished in the Second Temple period. Another interesting feature of the colony is a temple that contained a full sacrificial cult. From what can be reconstructed from the papyri, the temple served one main god, known by the name of Yahu or Yaho, another name for the more traditional Yahweh. Four other deities, including two female deities, were worshiped there as well. Oddly, no Hebrew Scriptures were found among the documents, but certain festivals, such as Passover and the Feast of Unleavened Bread, were observed. Again, the extant documents relating to worship might indicate something about the nature of ritual in the First Temple period. If the example of the Elephantine community holds true for the other Egyptian colonists, we can surmise that the Judahite refugees had relative freedom to govern themselves, to worship which deities they chose, and to maintain the traditions of their ancestors.

The biblical sources cast the choice for settlement in Egypt in a negative light. Jeremiah, for instance, denies refugees in Egypt the promise of a future:

> I am going to watch over them for harm and not for good; all the people of Judah who are in the land of Egypt shall perish by the sword and by famine, until no one is left. . . . This shall be a sign to you, says the LORD, that I am going to punish you in this place, in order that you may know that my words against you will surely be carried out. (Jer. 44: 27, 29; cf. 42:9–22; 44:14)

Though not as direct, Ezekiel predicts the utter destruction of Pharaoh and the country in his oracle against Egypt (chaps. 29–32). Indeed, the prophet makes it clear that the choice to flee to Egypt is a choice for death, because it is the reversal of the exodus from Egypt. Prophetic vitriol thus condemns the refugees in Egypt.

An interesting phenomenon in terms of religious thought transpired among the population that fled to Egypt. Jeremiah 44 portrays the entire family, including parents and children, participating in the religious worship of a female deity known only by an epithet "the queen of heaven." Although the identity of the "queen of heaven" remains disputed, growing biblical evidence favors the association of the goddess with Asherah. Asherah is most often found in the biblical text as a sacred tree or a wooden pole, but in a few texts she represents a full-fledged goddess (Day 1986; 2000). A growing number of scholars believe that she was a consort of Yahweh whose worship was accepted for a time in the Jerusalem temple. What is interesting is that when Jeremiah challenges the women over the worship of the queen of heaven, they reply that in their view the disasters occurred because cultic rituals in honor of the goddess were halted:

> As for the word that you have spoken to us in the name of the LORD, we are not going to listen to you. Instead, we will do everything that we have vowed, make offerings to the queen of heaven and pour out libations to her, just as we and our ancestors, our kings and our officials used to do, in the towns of Judah and in the streets of Jerusalem. We used to have plenty of food, and prospered, and saw no misfortune. But from the time we stopped making offerings to the queen of heaven and pouring out libations to her, we have lacked everything and have perished by the sword and by famine. (Jer. 44:16–18)

In their defense, the women include royalty and the general population among the practitioners of the cult of the goddess, thereby suggesting wide acceptance of ritual practices in her honor, even at the Jerusalem sanctuary. The movement to stamp out Asherah worship as one of the unorthodox cults could have taken place during Josiah's reforms (2 Kgs. 22–23), but could equally refer to an unspecified period such as during the siege of Jerusalem, when sacrifices would have been offered exclusively to the main deity of the city, Yahweh (M. Smith 1975). The reaction reveals a theological axiom in which the anger of a neglected deity causes repercussions in the human sphere. Consistent with Bob Becking's examination of reactions to disaster, the women insist on resuming the cult of the queen of heaven to assuage the wrath of the goddess.

The community that fled to Egypt after the fall of Jerusalem and the assassination of Gedaliah appears to have lived comfortably. During the sixth century BCE, the prophets directed scathing prophecies against them, condemning them to further divine judgment. Because reports of their religious activities in the Hebrew Bible served polemical purposes and may not correspond directly to the events themselves, it is difficult to know more about their circumstances in Egypt.

Babylon

During a series of military campaigns in Judah in the early part of the sixth century BCE, the Neo-Babylonians deported members of the community on at least three separate occasions: in 598 (2 Kgs. 24:14–16); in 587 (2 Kgs. 25:11, 21// Jer. 39:9; 52:15, 27), and in 582 (Jer. 52:30). There is no unbiased way to ascertain the exact number of deportees, because the biblical details recorded in 2 Kings 25 and Jeremiah disagree. Kings accounts only for the 598 exile, recording either 10,000 (2 Kgs. 24:14) or 8,000 (2 Kgs. 24:16) captives, while the sum of 4,600 listed in Jeremiah—3023 in 598 (Jer. 52:28), 832 in 587 (Jer. 52:29), and 745 in 582 (Jer. 52:30)—agrees with neither. Believing the numbers in Kings to be rounded figures suggesting a myriad of people, many accept the total number given in Jeremiah. As this figure probably includes only the male members of the community, it is multiplied by 4 or 5 (in line with average family sizes of the day) to arrive at 20,000–25,000 exiles relocated to Babylon (for further discussion, see Albertz 2003: 74–90). As we do not have accurate population figures for the time, it is difficult to assess what percentage of the inhabitants this amount represents. What is clear is that the community members reported to have been taken by the Babylonians represented the social, political, and religious leadership of the country. In fact, the biblical literature lists royalty, priests, artisans, craftsmen, and soldiers—in essence, the population of Jerusalem. Although the exact number of deportees remains unknown, the loss of influential members of society would have been keenly felt in Judah.

The day-to-day life of the exiles is relatively unknown, as there is little firsthand documentation about it outside of the biblical material, which itself says little about the exilic situation. Biblical texts thought to stem from a setting in Babylon during the sixth century include Isaiah 40–55, Jeremiah, Ezekiel, and Psalm 137 (perhaps also an edition of the Deuteronomistic History). From this material emerges a rather incomplete picture of the king and royal family located in the capital (2 Kgs. 25:27–30; Jer. 52:31–33), other exiles settled together along the canals of the Euphrates, with Ezekiel in Tel Abib (not present day Tel Aviv) (Ezek. 1:3; 3:15; Ps. 137), and elders with positions of authority (Jeremiah and Ezekiel address the elders in Jer. 29:1; Ezek. 8:1; 14:1; 20:1, 3). Noting the roles of Daniel (chaps. 1, 6) and of Nehemiah in the Persian court (Neh.

1), some have suggested that exiles would have officiated in the Babylonian royal court. The prophet Isaiah is reported to have predicted the Neo-Babylonian defeat of Judah and the service of royal sons as eunuchs in the palace (2 Kgs. 20:18//Isa. 39:7).

The biblical portrayal has been confirmed to some extent by Babylonian records. Three cuneiform tablets from the sixth century BCE that speak of the "villages of the Judahites" have recently come to light. They confirm the settlement of the deportees from Judah together in enclaves in the Babylon-Borsippa region and the business affairs in which they participated (Joannès and Lemaire 1999; Pearce 2006). In addition, documents termed the Weidner texts provide details of the amount of food and drink allotted to the king and his family while under house arrest. Finally, a cache of business contracts related to a prominent family, called the Murashu Documents, includes the names and occupations of Jews in Babylon from the fifth century into the fourth (Coogan 1974). These business documents show that Judahites were engaged in business affairs in Babylon and participated in farming and other agricultural pursuits. They seem to have had relative freedom to go about their affairs. When considering the Murashu archive, one should bear in mind that the documents date from well into the Persian period of rule and refer to Judahite communities further afield than those attested in the Babylonian records. As such, they may not indicate what exilic life was like a century earlier under the Babylonians.

In order to flesh out the relatively scanty details, interpreters have resorted to comparisons with Neo-Assyrian practices (cf. Oded 1979). From Neo-Assyrian tablets about the treatment of prisoners of war, it is possible to suggest that military leaders were conscripted into the Babylonian army, artisans were employed in building projects, and some were used as corvée labor to work on the king's building projects. The practice of deportation by empires known from iconography, inscriptions, and records provides another avenue of discussion. Deportation was a punitive response enacted by ruling states for treaty violations. Its use as a martial tactic can be traced to the important ruling powers of the ancient Near East, including the Egyptians, Hittites, Babylonians, and Persians, but it was perfected as a tactic by the Assyrians. Whole families were deported and resettled elsewhere in the empire. Chains were used on occasion, and pack animals with supplies accompanied the prisoners of war. In cuneiform texts, regulations about the treatment of prisoners were in place to curtail harsh treatment by soldiers and overseers. Deportation was used as a tactic of war to remove any incentive to return to the homeland

and to encourage settlement and integration in the empire. When considering the more plentiful Assyrian evidence of deportation as a martial tactic, it is important to bear in mind that in at least two instances the Neo-Babylonians departed from the practices of their predecessors: they settled deportees in national enclaves rather than exchanging populations, and deportees were relocated to the Babylonian heartland.

Daniel Smith(-Christopher) has sought to shed light on the rather benign portrait of exilic experience so often encountered in reconstructions of the period through a comparative anthropological and sociological study (1989; 2002).[3] In his reconstruction of the Babylonian exile, Smith-Christopher examined situations of forced relocation in more recent times (the internment camps of Japanese in America in World War II, for example). Through his comparison, Smith-Christopher has revealed more fully the human toll and interpretative response that resulted from the loss of family members, material possessions, land, and societal status. Moreover, he has placed stress on the physical demands of forced relocation across hundreds of miles as well as the emotional impact of witnessing the collapse of a nation and the suffering of friends, neighbors, and compatriots while in the homeland and en route to Babylon. Finally, he draws attention to the use of terms like "bondage" and "imprisonment" in the literature of the period and beyond. In spite of being allowed limited amounts of freedom in Babylon, the *golah* community existed as a minority identity among foreigners in a sophisticated and unfamiliar culture.[4] Suggestive of the depth of anger, grief, and despair is Psalm 137 (vv. 1–4, 7–9):

> By the rivers of Babylon—
>> there we sat down and there we wept
>> when we remembered Zion.
> On the willows there
>> we hung up our harps.
> For there our captors
>> asked us for songs,
> and our tormentors asked for mirth, saying,
>> "Sing us one of the songs of Zion!"

3. Smith now publishes as Smith-Christopher, but his monograph has been published under the former name.
4. One minor criticism of Smith-Christopher's emphasis on the hardship of exile is that he discounts Barstad's work on the empty land (1996) by suggesting that the approach is overstated and detracts from an awareness of exilic existence (2002: 45–49). It is possible to accept both continued existence in the homeland in conditions greater than on a subsistence level and a rigorous quality of life in Babylonia. The two are not mutually exclusive, and much light can be shed through consideration of both historical realities.

How could we sing the LORD's song
  in a foreign land? . . .
Remember, O LORD, against the Edomites
  the day of Jerusalem's fall,
how they said, "Tear it down! Tear it down!
  Down to its foundations!"
O daughter Babylon, you devastator!
  Happy shall they be who pay you back
  what you have done to us!
Happy shall they be who take your little ones
  and dash them against the rock!

In addition to feelings of anger and revenge, there was a sense of resignation. In Ezekiel 37:11 the community laments, "Our bones are dried up, and our hope is lost: we are cut off completely."

In Babylon, the community was faced with great loss: the loss of the homeland, the loss of leadership, the loss of cultural factors, the loss of the temple, and the loss of family members. Cast among a number of other peoples also removed from their homeland to Babylon, Judah's elite reassessed their religion and community. The fact that the Judahites were relocated together in communities enabled them to adapt creatively to their situation by establishing strategies to foster social cohesion and group identity. Smith-Christopher's study of modern situations of similar circumstances sheds light on how the exiles responded to the rupture in their world. Wrested from the familiar, they made changes in their conceptions of governance, society, and religion:

> The loss of the monarchy as the central political authority led to the rise of decentralized forms of organization that followed kinship lines, with the elders assuming leadership roles.
>
> On a social level, the loss of statehood forced the Judahites to be in constant contact with other nationalities. Two moves were made to provide a means to assess this new cosmopolitan situation. First, since membership of one's own group could no longer be taken for granted, outward signs that provided a sense of social identity and religious confession assumed greater significance as a guarantee of personal identity. For example, increased importance was ascribed to circumcision as a physical representation of being part of a special community. Second, the encounter with Babylon necessitated theological reassessment about the relation of foreign peoples to ancient Israel and

its deity. The conception of Yahweh as a universal god, a god of all peoples, came to the fore during this period. Contact with foreigners thus resulted in theological interpretation that fluctuated between particularism and universalism.

On a religious level, the loss of the temple as a center for cultic activity and as a place of worship resulted in a reformulation of how to access Yahweh in a foreign land. A belief in the mobility of Yahweh arose during this period. Until the fall of the temple, it was understood that Yahweh's presence resided in the Holy of Holies (Clements 1965). In addition, an intimate relationship with the deity is made available through prayer. The rabbis associate the beginning of prayer with Hannah, the mother of Samuel, who was the first person in the Hebrew Bible said to pray within her heart. After the destruction of the temple by the Romans in 70 CE, the rabbis considered prayer the equivalent of sacrificial worship. Prayers were made at times when sacrifices would have been offered at the temple. There is no evidence that the tradition linking Hannah with personal prayer occurred as early as the sixth century BCE, but the emphasis on the Jerusalem sanctuary as a place of prayer in 1 Kings 8, as well as Jeremiah's lesson to the exiles that Yahweh will hear their prayer wherever they reside (Jer. 29:12–14), is suggestive of a shift in thought toward personal piety.

In the face of tragedy and uncertainty, the religion of ancient Israel proved adaptive and transformative as it considered how one could be a Judahite in relationship with Yahweh outside of the land of Judah.

FROM DISASTER TO HOPE

The sixth century marked a great watershed in the historical, social, and religious life of Judah. A great rupture occurred in the political and religious establishment. The community was fragmented, with a population in the homeland recovering in the region north of Jerusalem, a community in Babylon settled in enclaves, and refugees scattered in Egypt and elsewhere.

As we shall see in the following chapters, these social, historical, and geographical circumstances provide the backdrop against which great literary activity took place, both recording the tragedy and confronting its challenges. Biblical scholars and historians tend to divide the sixth century into two time frames: an early period of destruction and desolation (587–550) and a later period of optimism and renewal (550–515). Soon after the fall of the temple the biblical outlook remains dark, as it focuses on recording the disaster and recounting grief and loss. In laments and the Deuteronomistic History there is little hope for a future beyond tragedy. After the shock of the downfall, Jeremiah and Ezekiel explained the disaster and provided a vision beyond it. Then, toward the close of the templeless age, Isaiah 40–55 and Ezekiel 40–48 sensed a shift in divine intentions and provided the theological impetus for return. Subsequently, the prophetic activity of Haggai and Zechariah spoke of communal preparation and response. Finally, the law in Leviticus 17–26 (the Holiness Code) clarified ways to restore and maintain covenant relations with Yahweh.

CHAPTER 2

The Aftermath of Disaster: I

Lamentation

There were two ways to mark the tragedy of the sixth-century catastrophe in the immediate aftermath. One was to mourn it, and another was to record it. Among the literature produced during the templeless age, some elicits little hope for a future beyond disaster. This literature primarily consists of psalms and laments, including the book of Lamentations. A lengthy historical overview called the Deuteronomistic History, which lacks a clear expression of hope in its conclusion and exemplifies this type of response, will be dealt with in the next chapter.

MOURNING AND WORSHIP

Tragedy on the scale that struck Judah at the beginning of the sixth century BCE resulted in a flood of emotions that can be profitably compared to the experience of the death of a loved one and may have entailed stages of grief: shock, disbelief, anger, and acceptance (Reimer 2002). In the ancient world, communities developed a series of mourning rituals to express anguish. Mesopotamian, Egyptian, and Canaanite texts have preserved a rich record of mourning rites assumed by ancient peoples after the destruction of a city or temple. Mesopotamian examples known collectively as the Sumerian and Mesopotamian City Laments appear in language, tone, and themes quite similar to the book of Lamentations in the Hebrew Bible (Dobbs-Allsopp 1993; *COS* vol. 1).

Examples of lamentation occur also in Canaanite literature. In a Canaanite poem the supreme god of the Ugaritic pantheon, El, laments the death of his son, Baal:

> Then El the kind, the compassionate, descends from the throne
> and sits on the footstool. . . . He strews stalks of mourning on his
> head, the dust in which he wallows on his pate. His clothing he
> tears, down to the loincloth, his skin he bruises with a rock by
> pounding, with a razor he cuts his beard and whiskers. . . . He
> raises his voice and shouts: "Baal is dead: What will happen to
> the people?" (Herdner 1963: 5.6.11–25)

Death or destruction resulted in a series of mourning rituals like those
assumed by El: the strewing of dirt, ashes, or dry stalks on the head; the
rending of clothing; shaving; cutting the body; loud wailing; and fasting.
Biblical portrayals of mourning rituals contain similar images, such as
those in Job 1–3 (see Olyan 2004). In fact, the tradition of mourning has
a long history in the Hebrew Bible. As Paul Ferris has shown in his examination of the setting and form of the communal laments, the Israelites
called a fast when routed by the Benjamites (Judg. 20:26) and the community entered into a period of lamentation after the death of Saul
(1 Sam. 31) (Ferris 1992). On this topic in particular, Xuan Pham has considered ancient Near Eastern mourning ceremonies in conjunction with
the biblical texts in Lamentations and Isaiah 51:9–52:2 (1999). She argues
that they have a discernible ritual through which a comforter brings relief
to the grief stricken. The people who had witnessed the ignoble collapse
of Jerusalem and the frightful events of the battle or those who had even
heard about it, participated in established rites to express their grief.

The community also voiced its despair in worship. There are examples
of worship continuing after the destruction of a city or temple elsewhere
in the ancient Near East. In Babylon, for instance, after the destruction of
the House of Sin—that is, the temple of the moon god—the high priest-
ess, Adad-Guppi (the mother of Nabonidus, king of Babylon) describes
in an autobiographical account her continued service among the ruins
and the mourning rituals she observed (Longman 1997). Similarly, the
Jews at Elephantine lamented the loss of their temple for roughly three
years after its razing until its reconstruction (Porten 1968: 289–93; 1996:
139–47). On the basis of analogies elsewhere, most scholars believe that
an organized cult provided a vehicle for Yahwistic worship by the people
who remained in Judah after 587. In the first place, the abundant city
laments from Sumer and Mesopotamia attest to liturgical pieces com-
posed to mourn the loss of cities and temples and provide a parallel to the
biblical Lamentations. Assyriologists have pointed out that these liturgical formulations tend to be used at the time of the reconstruction of the

temple and use hyperbolic language in order to entice the deity to return and bless the project. Although the laments were used in a ceremony marking repairs to or even the dedication of the temple, they contain language that was clearly suitable for use by mourners. As such they could have been used after the destruction of the temple or the city and reframed subsequently for use at a ceremony of dedication.

The imperial overseers certainly had an interest in allowing for the renewal of religious activity. In the conquest of Assyria, the Neo-Babylonians acted in a way that might parallel the situation in Judah. Before the final defeat of Assyria by the capture of Nineveh in 612, Babylon established an administrative center in Dur-Katlimmu, to the south of the capital. There, Nebuchadnezzar supported the rebuilding of a temple to Ashur, Assyria's main God. In Judah, Oded Lipschits (2005) has shown that the Babylonians had established Mizpah as an administrative center before the fall of Jerusalem, but there is no evidence that they invested any funds in the region or rebuilt a temple there. While there is no evidence yet of a temple in the region of Benjamin to the north of Jerusalem, it is certainly a possibility, given Babylonian attempts to generate stability in the region. That a sanctuary had been established has been argued on other grounds (see below).

The likelihood of the renewal of worship is supported by the passage in Jeremiah 41:4–5, in which pilgrims travel to the house of the LORD (*beth Yahweh*) bearing grain and incense offering:

> On the day after the murder of Gedaliah, before anyone knew of it, eighty men arrived from Shechem and Shiloh and Samaria, with their beards shaved and their clothes torn, and their bodies gashed, bringing grain offerings and incense to present at the house of the LORD.

The "house of the LORD" or the "house of God" (*beth elohim*) is an idiom that refers to the temple in Jerusalem. Because the men have assumed the appearance of mourning and bear only grain offerings and incense, it is reasonable to suppose that the destination is the ruined sanctuary in Jerusalem. It is significant that they do not have a sacrificial offering, as meat would not be appropriate on a broken—and therefore defiled—altar. Because the use of "*beth Yahweh*" with reference to the temple is ambiguous, Joseph Blenkinsopp has argued that it points to a sanctuary set up in or near the newly established regional capital at Mizpah. It is interesting that the Jeremiah passage does not refer to the location of the temple and the men are detoured in the vicinity of Mizpah by Ishmael:

"And Ishmael son of Nethaniah came out from Mizpah to meet them, weeping as he came. As he met them, he said to them, 'Come to Gedaliah son of Ahikam'" (Jer. 41:6).

The expression "*beth Yahweh*" usually means the Jerusalem temple, but it can be used with reference to other sacred sites such as general cultic areas (Exod. 23:19; 34:26; Josh. 6:26) and the Shiloh sanctuary when it housed the ark of the covenant (1 Sam. 1:24; 3:15; 2 Sam. 12:20). As compelling as it might be to understand an allusion to a sanctuary in Bethel here, there are several reasons to believe that it denotes the temple in Jerusalem. In the narratives recalling the fall of Jerusalem, the temple is called *beth Yahweh* (2 Kgs. 25:9, 13//Jer. 52:13, 17). Moreover, after the intention is made to build a temple in Jerusalem in 1 Kings 3, the designation is no longer used for any other sanctuary. Finally, Jeremiah uses this terminology only with reference to the Jerusalem temple (twenty-nine times). Even when the destruction of Shiloh is mentioned as an analogy to Jerusalem, neither Jeremiah nor the people speak of the cultic site that existed there (Jer. 7:14; 26:6, 9). Consistent with other literature of the period, *beth Yahweh* in Jeremiah 41 designates the Jerusalem temple. The operation of another sanctuary during the Neo-Babylonian period is not out of the question, but it is not possible to understand the Jeremiah reference this way. The text shows that continued worship was available. Lipschits has suggested further that Jeremiah 41:1–5 is better understood as an indication that spontaneous and sporadic worship took place at the temple site, rather than organized and regular ritual (2001; 2005).

A third indication that worship continued during the sixth century is found in the prophecies associated with Zechariah 1–8, which are dated by a chronological framework to the years 520–518. In an oracle from the deity, Zechariah remarks that the people had been observing fasts in the years prior to his prophecy: "Say to all the people of the land and the priests: When you fasted and lamented in the fifth month and in the seventh, for these seventy years, was it for me that you fasted?" (Zech. 7:5). The dates he mentions place the origin of ritual activity at the time of the destruction of the Jerusalem sanctuary.

Finally, the amount of attention in the literature of this period to religious practice makes the existence of ritual observance in Judah and Babylon (perhaps even in Egypt) likely. The literature of the templeless age is concerned to a large extent with the issue of worship, both heterodox and orthodox. The impression provided by the biblical writers certainly suggests that a great deal of illicit worship took place. In historiography and prophecy the issue of idolatry comes repeatedly to the fore. The

Deuteronomistic History (DtrH) places a great deal of the blame for the loss of the kingdom and homeland on what it considers to be inappropriate religious practices. Like DtrH, the prophets Jeremiah and Ezekiel condemn what they consider to be idolatrous cultic practices and use their existence in Judah, even on the temple mount, to explain the downfall of the kingdom. Moreover, Jeremiah condemns the community in Egypt for the persistence of the cult of the queen of heaven (Jer. 44). One of the necessary components of the restoration of Jerusalem in Ezekiel's vision (chaps. 40–48) is, therefore, the purification of the temple. Another prophet of the exile, Deutero-Isaiah (Isa. 40–55), attributes little blame for the disaster (Isa. 42:24–25; 43:27–28) but contains lengthy passages about the evils of false worship and the inefficacy of idols themselves, in polemical passages and trial speeches (chaps. 40–48).

In fact, one area of continuity between the final years of the monarchy and the early Second Temple period is that the worship of other deities, either in distinction to or in conjunction with the worship of Yahweh, took place. Prophetic angst at unorthodox religious practice does not cease with the return of the exiles to the land. Toward the end of the templeless age, the vision sequence of Zechariah 1–8 contains passages about purification, with one having to do with the return of a goddess to Babylon (Zech. 5:1–11). Moreover, sometime after the reconstruction of the temple, Trito-Isaiah attributes the failure of Deutero-Isaiah's predictions of divine salvation and restoration to materialize to the continued observance of rituals in honor of deities other than Yahweh (Isa. 57:3–13; 65:3–4, 11; 66:3, 17).

The literature of the templeless age shows increased concern to eradicate religious practice for any deity other than Yahweh. The intensity of interest and the widespread attestation of what was considered heterodox practice in some circles suggest that during the templeless age, a number of Judahites (whether in Judah or on foreign soil) turned to the worship of Baal, Asherah, the host of heaven, and idols, either in distinction to or in addition to the worship of Yahweh (Middlemas 2005a: 72–121). The condemnation of the practices in Jeremiah, Ezekiel, Deutero-Isaiah, the Deuteronomistic History, and elsewhere sought to persuade worshipers to turn wholeheartedly to Yahwistic practice by linking the fall of the kingdom to religious malpractice. Deuteronomic belief, with its worldview adopted from the book of Deuteronomy, which promised blessing for covenant obedience and destruction for disloyalty, became the dominant religious expression of the time. The underlying principle of Deuteronomic thought is the worship of Yahweh alone. The Yahwistic religion is in transition: there is a discernible shift from Yahwisms—a variety of ways to worship Yahweh and an understanding of Yahweh as the chief god in a pantheon (monolatry)—to monotheism—service to and acknowledgment of one and only one God (Edelman 1995). In conjunction with this shift, a variety of ways to worship Yahweh properly came to the foreground. One significant vehicle of expression would most certainly have been prayer.

Jeremiah 41:1–5 locates one possible site of worship in the templeless age at the ruins of the Jerusalem temple. Another possible site for more regular ritual observance is a sanctuary in the Benjamin region to the north of Jerusalem, in Mizpah or Bethel. According to biblical tradition, Bethel had a long history as a sacred site; Abraham and Jacob established altars there. It would not be in the interest of the biblical writers to mention a sacred center outside of Jerusalem, but there is one text that surely hints at the probability of cultic observance at Bethel during the Neo-Babylonian period. During the period of time in which Zechariah prophesied, a delegation is sent from Bethel to Jerusalem concerning a priestly interpretation:

> Now Bethel sent Sharezer and Regem-melech and their men, to entreat the favor of the Lord, and to ask the priests of the house of the Lord of hosts and the prophets, "Should I mourn and practice abstinence in the fifth month, as I have done for so many years?" (Zech. 7:2–3)

The NRSV contains the translation "Now the people of Bethel sent," but Bethel as the subject is in dispute, due to the lack of any indication of the direct object of the verb. Other arguments have favored Bethel as the location to which the men are sent (Blenkinsopp 1998; 2003; 2002: 425–26) or that Bethel-sharezer is the name of a royal official who sends a delegation (Edelman 2005: 91–92). The principles of Hebrew syntax argue against the former. The latter is based on speculation (Wellhausen 1898: 186), presumably confirmed by Hyatt (1937), but the evidence adduced is based on a single reference in an Akkadian text whose translation is under dispute (Hyatt 1937: 390). Moreover, Sharezer as a proper name is attested in the Hebrew Bible, where it is found as the name of one of Sennacherib's children, who assassinated him after his failed assault on Jerusalem (2 Kgs. 19:37//Isa. 37:38). Finally, of the seventy-five occurrences of Bethel in the Hebrew Bible, it is never used as the element of a name (see BDB: 110–11). It is unlikely that Bethel-sharezer represents a proper name in this text.

Normal Hebrew syntax provides some illumination, as the word order in the Hebrew text is consistent with Bethel as the subject. Furthermore, place names, such as Egypt, can stand for the people (BDB: 595). The city of Gilgal appears to stand for its populace when it is spoken of as going into exile in Amos 5:5.[1] In texts stemming from the sixth century BCE, the cities of Jerusalem, Babylon, and Samaria are personified and most assuredly represent their inhabitants (Isa. 49; Jer. 50–51; Ezek. 16, 23; Lam. 1:12–22; 2:20–22, et al.). These types of references point to the use of "Bethel" for its inhabitants, "Bethelians" or "the people of Bethel." Although many commentators accept Bethel as the subject of the verb "to send" (Ackroyd 1994: 206–9; Meyers and Meyers 1987: 382; Hoffman 2003: 200–202), they have failed to understand its significance in the context. After the return of some of the exiles to Judah, sacred authority would shift to Jerusalem, the old political and religious capital. The text indicates that priests in Bethel inquired about a cultic matter. The collection of visions and oracles in Zechariah 1–8 serves a unified purpose: to reassert the place of Jerusalem as the center of the entire world. Zechariah 7:2–3 portrays the transfer of religious authority to Jerusalem, in keeping with this message. The likelihood of there being a provisional sanctuary set up to the north of Jerusalem increases when one considers Blenkinsopp's observation that a series of allusions to the importance of Mizpah (Judg. 20–21; 1 Sam. 7:5–6, 11–12; 10:17) entered the tradition after the collapse of Jerusalem.

One essential feature of life in the ancient world was religion. No matter how limited, cultic worship must have continued in Judah. By analogy some type of religious observance could have taken place among the exiles in Babylon. A consideration of biblical literature from this period makes this more likely. During King Solomon's speech dedicating the first temple, verses are added that appear to account for a situation in which the sanctuary in Jerusalem was not operative. There the temple is called a house of prayer for all peoples. In the course of his dedication speech, King Solomon indicates different situations that would make prayer in the Jerusalem temple appropriate: defeat in battle (1 Kgs. 8:33–34); drought (vv. 35–36); other disasters such as famine, plague, blight, and locusts (vv. 37–40); and captivity (vv. 46–50) (Ferris 1992: 106–8). Moreover, liturgical pieces such as Psalm 137 and Isaiah 51:19 belong to the *golah* community and could stem from settings in worship.

---

1. Bethel is parallel to Gilgal, which suggests that it functions in a similar way.

Finally, the fast days mentioned in Zechariah 8:18–19 include those for the king and palace. It is thought that the community exiled to Babylon would have had a special desire to lament the loss of the king, as he had been deported with them. The book of Ezekiel—widely agreed to have been written in Babylon—provides some support for this view, as its dating sequence is numbered according to the regnal years of King Jehoiachin, who was exiled in the first Babylonian deportation.

During the templeless age, the Judahites (whether in the homeland or on foreign soil) continued their Yahwistic and non-Yahwistic practices of worship. Yahwistic worship is thought to be the setting for the production of laments to express dismay and despair. Religion provided a vehicle to allow a community to cope and move beyond catastrophe. Through long-established rituals, the community grieved its collective loss.

LITURGY AND LAMENTATION

The majority of liturgical literature from this period corresponds to a form-critical category known as the communal laments. Hermann Gunkel first organized biblical and extrabiblical liturgical pieces (mainly psalms) into categories based on whether or not they expressed a hymn or a lament, as well as whether they were spoken by an individual or plural voice (1928–33, ET 1998). The communal or national laments, a class that is made up of many of the psalms and includes Lamentations 5, share similar formulaic elements. These similarities suggested to Gunkel that the psalms were literary pieces that represented oral poems used in worship, that is, vestiges of earlier material later written down. His results were enriched by the studies of Sigmund Mowinckel (1962). Disagreeing with the literary emphasis of Gunkel, Mowinckel argued that these psalms represented actual songs used in ceremonies at the temple. He used the psalms to reconstruct what ceremonies would have been like in ancient Israel. Since the time of Gunkel and Mowinckel, then, it is commonplace to associate these psalms with ritual worship. It is believed that certain psalms reflect the continuation of prayer at the ruined temple. It is also likely that prayer took place in alternative sanctuaries established during the period.

According to Gunkel's criteria, the prayers of this period would be national or communal laments. Although it is notoriously difficult to associate many of the psalms with specific historical events or time periods, the national complaints are thought to be more readily attributable, due to recognizable historical details. As a genre, they exhibit a corporate response to a political disaster. They contain three basic elements: the lament, a confession of trust or certainty of a hearing, and an appeal. The lament section describes at variable length an event that has had dire consequences for the nation, such as a military defeat, the death of a king, or the desecration/destruction of the temple. In the confession of trust, the community speaks of reasons to trust the deity to intervene in the present distress by recounting events in the past when the deity acted on behalf of the people through either historical or cosmological events. This section corresponds loosely to Gunkel's "confidence of being heard" in that it serves as the axis of the poem by indicating reasons to believe that the lament will be answered, and in so doing provides the grounds for the appeal. The appeal corresponds to what is lamented. In it the community petitions the deity to come to the nation's rescue.

In spite of the fact that most of the laments associated with the templeless age have been classified as communal or national laments, other types of lamentations appear as well, including the communal dirge, penitential prayer, and mixed forms. Nancy Lee, who has worked on correspondences between the biblical book of Lamentations and the types of poetic literature that have arisen from situations of crisis throughout history (2002), has coined the phrase "communal dirge." Her category fits well with the long-held recognition that Lamentations 1, 2, and 4 contain language used to honor the dead in a funeral dirge, as well as communal lamentation. In addition, there are types of prayer that are best defined as penitential prayer. This genre is related to communal laments but has a lengthy confession of sin instead of the focus on the mournful present. A third genre represents a mixed form in which elements from various genres (individual lament, communal lament, and penitential prayer) have been combined.

Scholars attribute a varying number of laments to the templeless age. A conservative list includes Psalms 74, 79, 89, 102, 106, 137, Lamentations, and Isaiah 63:7–64:11.[2] With the exception of Psalm 137, they are thought to have their setting in life (*Sitz im Leben*) in worship services at the Jerusalem temple. A closer analysis of these texts makes definitive ascriptions of their provenance difficult, as they contain stereotypical language and a variety of themes. Many of the themes covered suit a templeless context, but not a specific place of origin. The liturgical pieces divide into five categories: (1) the communal laments: immediate reac-

---

2. Psalm 44 is frequently included in a list of psalms from this period, but its historical details are vague and relate better to the defeat of a king in battle (Craigie 2002: 330–35).

tions (Pss. 79 and 137); (2) the communal laments: prayer and petitions (Pss. 74 and 89 and Lam. 5); (3) the communal dirge (Lam. 1, 2, and 4); (4) penitential prayer (Ps. 106 and Isa. 63:7–64:11; cf. Neh. 9);[3] and (5) mixed forms (Ps. 102 and Lam. 3).

Communal Laments: Immediate Reactions—Psalms 79 and 137

Within the category of the communal laments, Psalms 79 and 137 deserve separate treatment because they do not include a fully expressed section about reasons to trust in the deity's future action. The language employed is caustic, angry, and frustrated.

Psalm 79—A people despised by the nations. Generally agreed to hail from the templeless age, due to the concern with the desecration of the sanctuary, the psalm divides into two sections: a short lament (vv. 1–5) followed by a series of petitions calling for the deity to vindicate the distressed community (vv. 6–13). In the lament, the people cry out over foreign invasion, the defilement, if not the destruction, of the Jerusalem temple, the ruination of Jerusalem, the murder of its inhabitants, and their subsequent disgrace. The lament leads directly into an appeal for divine assistance (vv. 6–12) and closes with a vow of praise (v. 13). Unlike other laments of this period, Psalm 79 contains no confession of trust or a separate account of the past actions of Yahweh that encourages belief in future saving deeds.

The lack of a clear confession of trust, however, does not exclude belief in the saving power of Yahweh. Throughout the lament, the community identifies itself as the people of Yahweh, using language evocative of the covenant such as "Jacob" (v. 7), "servants" (vv. 2, 10), "your faithful" (v. 2; lit. "holy ones"), "your people" (v. 13), and "the flock of your pasture" (v. 13). The lamenters are the community of Yahweh, and the deity's reputation is inextricably linked to their fate.

Psalm 137—A people scattered and shattered. Like Psalm 79, Psalm 137 contains no separate confession of trust in which the people outline their reasons for belief in divine assistance. It contains a vivid response to disaster, with the lament of a people exiled to Babylon in disgrace (vv. 1–4), followed by an appeal for the deity's assistance in the language of a curse (vv. 5–6) and of revenge (vv. 7–9). Because of the insertion of a curse form into a communal complaint, Gunkel classified this psalm as a mixed

---

3. Nehemiah 9 is another example of this genre, but its attribution to the sixth century BCE is disputed. Some date it to the Second Temple period (Coates 1968: 241–48; Boda 1999), while Williamson 1985 includes it among the laments of the sixth century BCE. As its date of origin requires additional thought, it has not been included, but the reader is referred to its possible inclusion.

form and dated it to the Second Temple period. The psalm certainly has complaint elements (see Westermann 1981: 52–64; Allen 2002: 234–43) but is not necessarily later than the rebuilding of the temple (Allen 2002: 239). The last of the Songs of Zion (Pss. 46, 48, 76), it is certainly an odd way to end this group of psalms, which tend to sing about pilgrimage to Zion, the celebration of the temple mount, the glorification of the deity, and the subjugation of the enemy. In Psalm 137, the people lament the miserable loss of Zion, the defeat of the nation, and the victory of the enemy. Rather than praise God, they appeal for revenge.

Psalms 79 and 137 appear to reflect immediate reactions to disaster. The people lament deportation to Babylon (Ps. 137) as well as the destruction of the temple and the loss of the land (Ps. 79). These prayers contain heartfelt expressions of anger, dismay, frustration, and terror. Instead of theological formulation or explanation, there is bitter agony as well as the direct and urgent appeal for divine help.

Communal Laments: Petitions and Prayers—Psalms 74, 89; Lamentations 5

The poems in this section are those that fall most readily into the category of communal or national laments. Communal laments are complaints from the perspective of the plural "we" or the community. They contain the three elements typical of national laments: the lament proper, a confession of trust, and an appeal.

Psalm 74—Lament for the destroyed temple. This psalm includes various details suggestive of the destruction of Jerusalem, the temple, and its environs in 587. The community laments that the enemy has destroyed everything within the sanctuary (v. 3), stood triumphant within it (v. 4), hacked at its edifice (vv. 5–6), burned it to the ground (v. 7a), and profaned it (v. 7b). In addition to the destructive activities wrought in the temple, the invaders have burned all the meeting places of God in the land (v. 8). Psalm 74 has a tripartite structure: a lengthy lament concerned with how long the temple will remain defiled and ruined (vv. 1–11), a hymnic confession of trust in which the actions of Yahweh as king and creator are recounted (vv. 12–17), and an appeal to Yahweh to intervene to overturn the present distress (vv. 18–23). The confession of trust contains a mythic sequence that recalls a primordial time when the deity established his kingship by vanquishing chaos, conceived of as the sea monster, and when the deity created the foundations of the earth by breaking the dams of the deep.

Psalm 89—Lament for the house of David. Although Gunkel initially included Psalm 89 with the royal laments, it is more fitting that it is included in the communal laments of this period, because of the lament over the deity's abrogation of the Davidic covenant in verses 39–46. In its final form it appears to contain a royal psalm from the First Temple period adapted to a lamentation following the fall of Jerusalem. Although most interpreters now regard it as a single literary unit for purposes of interpretation (see the review of scholarship in Heim 1998 and Mitchell 2005), Dumortier has argued that the royal psalm (vv. 2–5, 20–38) and a cosmogonic myth (vv. 6–19) were actually written as a single literary unit (1972). As no other occasion in the history of Judah than that of the sub-jugation of Jerusalem in 587 would lament the loss of the Davidic king, the psalm surely belongs to this period. The three formal elements typical of laments appear: a hymnic recital that functions as the confession of trust (vv. 2–38), the lament (vv. 39–46), and the appeal (vv. 47–52). In the confession of trust the cosmic myth of Yahweh's battle with the sea is joined to the historical choice of David as king. The combination of myth and history provides a distinctive expression of confidence in divine intervention in the future.

Lamentations 5—Lament over the dire present. The fifth chapter of Lamentations has long been thought to contain one of the purist examples of a communal lament in the Hebrew Bible. It has a long litany of complaint in verses 1–18, where the people highlight suffering in evocative language (their own suffering, the desolate state of the temple, and the loss of the king); an abbreviated confession of trust affirming faith in the longevity and the kingship of the deity (v. 19); and an appeal (vv. 20–22), where a question mark hangs over whether Yahweh will choose to redeem. When compared to the communal laments of the Psalter, Lamentations 5 has two distinctive features. In the first place, it contains an overview of the present abominable state of affairs that in the depth of detail and the sheer number of lines is unlike other examples of its genre. Secondly, the poem ends on a note of uncertainty. Instead of the normal appeal that asserts praiseworthy attributes of the deity, it concludes with a question mark over the divine purposes for this people.

The final verses conclude the fifth lament, as well as the entire collection of Lamentations, on a note of uncertainty. This uncertainty is clear in the lament itself. In spite of the fact that the lament contains a confession of trust in that it turns to a secure reason to trust in the future salvific intervention of the deity ("You, O LORD, reign forever" [Lam. 5:19]), the lament by its focus on destruction has raised a question about the location of his rule. The communal lament of Lamentations 5, then, raises a concern over Yahweh's purposes for the people—will the deity choose to be in relation with this people again? The uncertainty comes to light through the agonizing ending, "unless you have utterly rejected us and remain angry with us beyond measure" (Lam. 5:22).

The communal or national laments of this period, as expressed in Psalms 74 and 89 and Lamentations 5, provide examples of how the community mourned its crisis. Particularly within the confession of trust, the community voiced its understanding of its deity. The confessions in the three examples differ remarkably. In Psalm 74, the community recounts Yahweh's victorious conquest of chaos portrayed as watery forces and as a sea monster. This myth appears in Psalm 89 as well, there combined with the deity's choice of the Davidic king. Yahweh's primordial rule links with that of an earthly ruler—joined are mythic and historical details. Finally, Lamentations 5 contains a rather brief confession of trust articulated as the attestation of Yahweh as king. There are no further details to clarify the context of the statement—whether it is to be understood within a mythic context (Yahweh became king by vanquishing the watery forces of chaos) or historical context (Yahweh has chosen Zion as the place for the divine presence or the king as the divine representative). In all three laments, the people evoke God's actions in the past that would be suggestive of forthcoming actions.

The Communal Dirge: Lamentations 1, 2, and 4

Three chapters of Lamentations are similar in structure, form, and theme. Chapters 1, 2, and 4 are alphabetic acrostics in which the consonants of the Hebrew alphabet introduce the first word of each verse. In addition, though classified by Gunkel as national funeral dirges, these chapters employ elements of the communal lament. The funeral dirge is a literary genre first intensively studied by Hedwig Jahnow (1923), who herself fell victim to persecution by the Nazis. Jahnow showed how this genre belongs to the funeral service and the language is akin to an elegy that mourns the dead. Claus Westermann qualified Jahnow's categorization of the funeral dirge by showing that it is only partially employed in these chapters of Lamentations (1994). Building on the work of Jahnow and Westermann, as well as on her own analysis of the poems of Lamentations, Lee has argued for new terminology that might be more appropriate—the communal dirge (2002). The first chapter contains the most numerous elements of the funeral dirge, but statements consistent with the lament appear. Gradually, in chapters 2 and 4 the mournful march of the dirge recedes as the language of lament increases (Linafelt 2000b: 75). The poems are directed to Yahweh, but rather than formulating lengthy statements about the positive attributes of the deity that offer hope, these chapters of Lamentations focus on the deity as an enemy of the people who has caused their distress. Although the ultimate source of the devastation is a divine one, the poets are equally aware of the role played by the Babylonians. The triumphant foe has acted as Yahweh's agent of destruction. The language used of their power is violent; the account of the entry into and desolation of the temple even verges on the language of rape. The sense of outrage and despair is not only directed outward. The poets of Lamentations grieve the present distress and highlight the reversal of fortunes. Jerusalem is a conquered city, the people are humiliated, the city and its citizens suffer.

Thematically, the three chapters are similar in that they focus on the catastrophe of 587 and mourn the ignoble collapse of Jerusalem and the violence wrought against its citizenry. Several different speaking voices capture in vivid detail the present and recent distress. An eyewitness narrator speaks in Lamentations 1:1–11, 2:1–19, and chapter 4. The city of Jerusalem, personified as a widowed and suffering woman, cries out in 1:12–22 and 2:20–22. Each voice laments in a litany of despair.

Penitential Prayer: Isaiah 63:7–64:11 and Psalm 106

Penitential prayers are similar to the communal laments in that a community prays together, recounting the history of their interaction with Yahweh. Isaiah 63:7–64:11 contains a historical recital that corresponds to the confession of trust in a communal lament, as well as a confession of sin that functions like a lament. In Psalm 106, the historical recital is combined with the confession of sin.

Isaiah 63:7–64:11—Lament over ongoing desolation. Often included among the communal laments, Isaiah 63:7–64:11 appears in Third or Trito-Isaiah (Isa. 56–66). Bernhard Duhm—noting differences in literary style, place, and theology within the book of Isaiah—argued persuasively for the existence of separate collections of oracles in Isa. 40–55 and 56–66. Isaiah 56–66 is widely agreed to date to the Second Temple period. It contains in chapters 60–62 oracles of pure joy like those of Isaiah 40–55, but it shows a concern for questions about who has access to the temple in the new age and why the promises of imminent salvation have failed to materialize (P. Smith 1995; Middlemas 2005b). Westermann, followed by many, has argued that the lament in Isaiah 63:7–64:11 stems from the templeless age and was recited along with other laments in ceremonies of the time (1969: 385–98). He includes it among the literature of the sixth century because of references that fit the period, such as the destruction of the temple (63:18; 64:10), the suggestion of foreign rule (63:19), the complete devastation of the city of Jerusalem and outlying areas (64:9), and the inactivity (64:6, 11) and anger of the deity (64:4, 8). Its placement after the singularly hopeful message of Isaiah 60–62 explains why Yahweh's salvific intervention has not taken place as expected. This lament, originally from the templeless age, was placed in its current position by a redactor in order to remind the audience of the disaster, because behavior that caused the ruination of the state continued (Smith 1995).

The poem has features that distinguish it from the communal laments studied so far. Instead of the threefold structure of lament, confession of trust, and appeal, Isaiah 63:7–64:11 contains a historical retrospect in which praise predominates (63:7–14), a confession of sin (63:15–64:6), and an appeal for salvation (64:7–11). The historical recital functions as a profession of trust while the confession of sin corresponds to the lament. Elements of lament are included in the confession (63:18, 19). It recounts the faithfulness of Yahweh in a litany of the deity's salvific actions in history, followed by a confession of sin that serves as the basis for an appeal for restoration. The fundamental belief in Yahweh's future intervention rests on memories of the exodus, wilderness wanderings, and entry into the land (vv. 6–14). Hope in this lament is based not on myth, but on the history of Yahweh's actions of redemption on behalf of the covenant people.

Psalm 106—A cultic prayer of repentance. Categorized by Gunkel as a communal lament, Psalm 106 includes elements of praise. Like Isaiah 63:7–64:11, the psalm contains a historical retrospect framed by praise. Most interpreters place its origin within the templeless age, but there are no firm historical indicators of its genesis there (see the review in Allen 2002: 44–56). Like the lament in Trito-Isaiah, Psalm 106 contains a lengthy historical recital of the exodus and wilderness traditions that highlights Yahweh's presence with the people in the past in spite of their repeated covenant failures. The psalm has three elements: the appeal (vv. 4–5, 47), the confession of trust (vv. 1–3, 48), and a lengthy confession of sin acting as the communal lament (vv. 6–46). In the confession of sin the people recount the ways they have rebelled against the covenant with Yahweh. Though Yahweh saved them in Egypt and led them forth through the Red Sea, they rebelled during their trek across the wilderness and upon entry into the promised land (Coates 1968: 227–30). In their retrospective view of history the people align themselves with their recalcitrant forebears. The community bears the burden of responsibility for the exile. In the appeal, they praise Yahweh and divine loyalty (*hesed*) to the covenant.

The penitential prayers from this period show a further adaptation of the basic form of the communal lament. Rather than being connected to language consistent with a funeral, historical retrospective focuses attention on the interactions of Yahweh and the people in the past. In Isaiah 63:7–64:11, the people separate the historical recital, which focused on Yahweh's continued provision in spite of human failing, from the confession of sin. Psalm 106 joined the historical recital with the confession of sin and showed the history of the people to be defined by rebellion. The origin of this distinctive type of prayer is unknown. The confession of sin in Psalm 106 draws on Deuteronomic thought but contains some details consistent with the Priestly work (for a helpful analysis of the motif of the rebellion in the wilderness, see Coates 1968).

Mixed Forms: Psalm 102 and Lamentations 3

Mixed forms are psalms in which various elements are combined, defying easy classification.

Psalm 102—Lament over the ruination of Jerusalem. Psalm 102 is very clearly an individual lament (see the heading and the individual's distress likened to an illness in vv. 3–11 and 23–24). Commonly it is included among the templeless laments because the individual's complaints have been joined with a communal concern for the restoration of Zion. More specifically, the individual leaves the impression that he/she is far from Judah, Zion is in ruins (v. 15), the people experience oppression (vv. 18, 21), but they maintain hope nonetheless in divine initiative to rebuild Zion (v. 17 in prophetic perfects) and the revelation of divine glory (vv. 16–17). Through the rehearsal of very personal pain, the community expresses its ongoing suffering over the ruins of Zion and the oppression of the covenant people (vv. 12–22). Like the communal laments, it has a series of complaints (vv. 3–11 and 23–24), an appeal (vv. 1–2), and confessions of trust (vv. 12–22 and 25–28). Upon closer inspection the confessions of trust exhibit an interesting development. Positive statements about the deity are linked with specific acts of restoration. The first one joins faith in the eternal rulership of Yahweh with plans to restore Zion while the second contrasts the agelessness and power of the creator deity with the ephemeral nature of human life, in order to point towards the restoration of his covenant people, here called "the children of your servants" (v. 28).

Included among the communal laments of the time, Psalm 102 evidences the intermingling of the complaint of the individual and the lament of the community. By utilizing elements of both genres, the psalmist draws attention to destruction and dramatizes it in a way that would urge the deity to take notice and act.

Lamentations 3—The suffering of the strong man as an example to every man. Like Lamentations 1, 2, and 4, chapter 3 is an alphabetic acrostic. However, its acrostic is more intense, as each consonant of the alphabet introduces three lines, which results in a poem with an impressive 66 verses. Furthermore, the lines are short, which produces a rather staccato effect that emphasises the urgent nature of the complaint. Gunkel classified Lamentations 3 as a mixed psalm because it contains features consistent with several different formal types: the individual complaint (vv. 1–21, 49–66), a communal lament/confession of sin (vv. 40–48), and a parenetic section (vv. 22–39) more akin to Wisdom literature than prayer. Although its placement within Lamentations implies a date shortly after the fall of the temple in 587 BCE, the combination of different formal elements suggests that it stems from a later period. It is concerned with the ruination of Jerusalem and shares some features with the final Suffering Servant passages in Isaiah 40–55 (Isa. 50:4–11; 52:13–53:12; see Willey 1997). There is no firm evidence for placing it outside of the templeless age (Middlemas 2006).

The constituent parts of the poem have been considered by Gunkel and Westermann, but only more recently has concern been raised about how it functions as the sum of its parts. Ulrich Berges recently considered it as the lament of Zion enacted in the restored temple (2004). However, it aligns more closely with literature of the templeless age. As such, it shows the community how to respond to disaster. When suffering (vv. 1–21), one should wait for the omnipotent and omniscient deity patiently, silently, and expectantly (vv. 22–39). The proper posture in crisis leads to the recognition of the part sin has played in separating the individual from God, and the community confesses its sin (vv. 40–48). Oriented correctly to the deity, the individual as representative of the community then resumes his lament with the understanding that Yahweh will fight for him (vv. 49–66). The poem fits well with the Deuteronomic emphasis on penitence and shows the community how to respond to crisis through highlighting the strong man as an example.

In poetry exhibiting mixed forms, the lament of an individual has been transformed to speak to a communal concern. In Psalm 102, the individual's illness is likened to the destruction of Jerusalem. The individual in Lamentations 3 provides the means for the community to confess its sin and restore a right posture before its deity. Throughout the templeless age, the laments take on a variety of forms to capture the situation, express grief, and move beyond the present with a renewed vision of the divine plan.

FINAL THOUGHTS ON THE LAMENTS OF THE TEMPLELESS AGE

In the liturgy and lamentation of this period the people bring to the attention of Yahweh quite a few different complaints: in Psalm 74, the community laments the loss of symbols of divine presence like the temple and prophecy; Psalm 79 bemoans destruction of the temple and of the people; and Isaiah 63:7–64:11 highlights the ruins of the city of Jerusalem. In distinction, Psalm 89 mourns the loss of the Davidic king while Psalm 106 speaks of the exile. The lament section of Psalm 102 focuses on the suffering of an individual, but it ultimately seeks the restoration of the temple. The book of Lamentations above all else highlights the human tragedy that accompanied war and its aftermath. The liturgical pieces assisted the grieving process of the community. In them the foundation traditions and ideologies of the society were shaped to calm chaotic circumstances, in order to make life in the aftermath of disaster bearable. Though frequently not valued as much as the historical accounts or prophetic literature, the prayers of the period deserve equal treatment. Beyond allowing a despairing people a faithful vehicle in which to grieve, they provide a means to understand the ability of religion to formulate identity and explain reality in the face of crisis.

The laments of the Neo-Babylonian period provide glimpses into the tragedy of a nation and the means taken to confront it and even move beyond it. They differ remarkably in the points they raise, the concerns they have, and even the language used. However, as a summary, they can be understood as contributing to the response to suffering on three levels: (1) the expression of grief, (2) an explanation for suffering, and (3) consideration of future possibilities.

The Expression of Grief

After the fall of Jerusalem the nation entered a period of mourning. The laments of the templeless age show the importance ascribed to the proclamation of distress. Grieving was never displayed as a solitary, private, or individual action. Rather, the community grieved together vocally in formal prayer to the deity.

The liturgy of this period revealed the validity of complaint or even protest. Psalms 79, 137, and Lamentations are powerful modes of expression. All use the language of prayer common in the temple to capture the depth of human tragedy and the very real human emotions of anger, dismay, heartbreak, and fear. No matter how caustic or unpleasant the message, the liturgy expressed the gamut of human experience within the setting of worship. Each prayer insisted urgently that Yahweh see and act. The psalms contain appeals to the deity for assistance related to the particular need expressed in the lament, but in Lamentations the emphasis is placed on vocalizing the painful present (Linafelt 2000a). In chapter 1, Lady Jerusalem interrupts the narrator twice, almost as a means of signifying that she is not dead and her need is urgent: "Look, O LORD, and see" (Lam. 1:9c, 11c). So urgent is her appeal that she interrupts the narrator to conclude the chapter (1:12–22). In the second chapter, she appears cowed under the suffering that has transpired. In response to her silence, the narrator presses her to cry out (2:18–19). Although she responds with a cry for revenge (vv. 20–22), her voice is not heard again in Lamentations. Instead, the community picks up her plea: "Look, O LORD and see" (5:1).

The laments surveyed poignantly portray in evocative language the human toll of the disaster. Every facet of Judah had been destroyed, including the assurance of divine presence and protection made available at the temple (Pss. 74 and 79), political stability ensured by the continuation of the Davidic line (Ps. 89), and the security of the nation (Pss. 102; 106; Isa. 63:7–64:11). The poems in Lamentations 1, 2, and 4 include the temple and the structures of the city among its concerns, but highlight in the most graphic language the human side of the tragedy. The poet uses a variety of means to emphasize the personal effects of institutional disaster, such as the motif of the reversal of fortune, the horrific depiction of famine, the city figured as a heartbroken woman, and the role of the enemies who exceeded their authority in their use of violence. The poet pictures human suffering on a divine scale. Lamentations 4 has the most consistent portrait of suffering with its agonizing portrayal of every member of society—women, men, the elderly, and children, rich and poor—bowed in the aftermath of war beneath the brunt of subjugation, disease, famine, and starvation. The poet represents the catastrophe in such graphic language to draw the attention of Yahweh to the plight that gripped the nation.

Finally, some of the laments of this period express doubt. In the book of Lamentations, there is no overt message of hope except in the third chapter, where a powerful expression of Yahweh's salvific characteristics appears. These optimistic verses are overrun by the tragedy that surrounds them—as the peaceful eye of a hurricane is engulfed by driving winds and torrential rain (Middlemas 2004). The book ends on a note of uncertainty that raises the question whether the deity will choose to be in relation with this people again (Lam. 5:21–22). Nowhere is there a question about the power or sovereignty of Yahweh. Instead, the people wonder whether Yahweh will honor the covenant and enter into a restorative relationship with them. The community's expression of acute suffering and doubt in prayer is one of the faithful ways it claimed the responsibility of its deity, asserted loyalty to Yahweh, and asked for restoration.

An Explanation of Suffering

The liturgy provides an answer to the palpable question, Why? In so doing, it serves the purpose of theodicy (explaining and defending the actions of the deity). In this way, the laments contain a dual focus on the actions of Yahweh and the efficacy of human responsibility.

The liturgy attributed the cause of the catastrophe to Yahweh. Contrary to other worldviews that might understand the downfall of a nation as the defeat of one deity by another, ancient Israel conceived of its circumstances as the result of the actions of Yahweh alone. Two portraits of the deity emerged in conjunction with this belief. In a helpful study of the psalms from this period, Craig Broyles has shown how the different confessions of trust appeal to two different understandings of the deity's behavior (1989). The first is that of a passive deity, who has withdrawn divine support from the covenant people (Ps. 74) or hidden the divine face (Ps. 102). The second acknowledges the intentionality of the deity by attributing the destruction to Yahweh's actions (Ps. 89; Lam. 1:12–22; 2). The two conceptions of Yahweh are interwoven in Lamentations 2:3: "He has cut down in fierce anger all the might of Israel; he has withdrawn his right hand from them in the face of the enemy; he has burned like a flaming fire in Jacob, consuming all around." In Lamentations the poet even designates Yahweh an enemy (Lam. 2:4–5, 22). Just as they understand their God to have been the driving force behind their magnificent collapse, they view the renewal of Yahweh's commitment as essential to the restoration of their status as the covenant people. The communal laments address Yahweh directly with urgent requests for divine intervention.

In addition to the recognition of divine causality, the community understood the correlation of the judging actions of the deity with their behavior. For them, Yahweh acted out the purposes as foretold by the prophets of the First Temple period:

> The LORD has done what he purposed,
>   [God] has carried out the his threat;
> as he ordained long ago,
>   he has demolished without pity.
>   *(Lam. 2:17)*

Rather than accuse the deity of injustice, the liturgy implied that the punishment for covenant disloyalty was well known. In addition, Yahweh's actions are explicable because the people sinned. The acknowledgment of the efficacy of sin became an important element in the laments of this period (e.g., Lam. 1:18, 20; Isa. 64:7–11; Ps. 106). Defining Yahweh's actions as a response to the wrongful behavior of covenant partner Israel is one way the literature of this time explained the crisis.

It should not go unnoticed in a summary of the thought of the liturgy of this period that clear explanations for the reasons for the disaster (divine response to human sin) appear alongside certain questions about the nature of the disaster itself. These are statements of disbelief that rest on the inexplicable. For instance, although the poets recognized the connection between human transgression and the ruination of Zion, Lamentations downplays the force of sin. The offense of the sin committed did not equal the amount of suffering experienced. As F. Dobbs-Allsopp has shown, the description of the efficacy of sin decreases its significance as an explanation for the disaster (1997). He points out that (1) sin is referred to relatively infrequently when compared to images of suffering, (2) there is a noticeable lack of specificity when references are made, and (3) some of the confessions of sin are intentionally undermined contextually (Lam. 1:18 when read in conjunction with 1:15, for example). There are acknowledgments of sin (1:8–9, 14, 18, 20) and even its greatness (4:6), but Lamentations repeatedly asserts that the punishment far outweighed the crime.

The way the significance of sin is downplayed in Lamentations suggests that in addition to explaining the actions of Yahweh, the poems serve to highlight the brutality of divine behavior. For example, in chapter 4, which concentrates almost exclusively on the graphic portrayal of human pain, there is no acknowledgment of sin at all. In Lamentations 2, where the poet contains an almost myopic focus on the destructive force of the deity (as divine warrior and as the authority for the invaders), there is only one statement of sin, and that refers to the failure of the prophets to make the people aware of their transgression (2:14). Rather than theodicy, then, the poems in Lamentations would more accurately be thought of as *theo-diabole*, accusations against the deity. Some evidence in support of this interpretation lies in the paraenetic section of the third chapter (Middlemas 2006). The wisdom verses appended to the lament of the individual counter accusations made against the deity in the rest of Lamentations—either directly, as in "the LORD will not reject forever" (3:31), "[God] does not willingly afflict or grieve anyone" (3:33), "Why should any who draw breath complain about the punishment of their sins?" (3:39), or indirectly. The poet refutes concerns raised by the community about its deity by favoring a description of Yahweh as divine savior rather than divine warrior (3:22–24, 31–39). Moreover, he emphasizes divine omniscience to contradict the implication that the failure of the deity to see the distress has led to its magnitude or longevity. Finally, he indicates the proper human response to disaster: to accept correction and to wait quietly and patiently for divine intervention (3:25–30).

Liturgical formulations from Judahite communities in the aftermath of 587 provided explanations for the disaster based on the precepts of the religion of ancient Israel. As the only deity, Yahweh became responsible for the disaster. The people, in disobeying the covenant with Yahweh, bore part of the responsibility for the execution of divine wrath. Nevertheless, the severity of what was regarded as punishment for unorthodox behavior remained inexplicable, and accusations against Yahweh emerged.

Consideration of Future Possibilities

In addition, the literature moves the orientation of the community toward the future. In so doing, it has to come to terms with traditions that seem unshakable. The literature calls into question the predominant ideology of the monarchical period, known as Zion theology, in particular. In Zion theology, associated with the choice of a place and the choice of a king (Hayes 1963), Yahweh is understood to have expressed his power and governance through historical events and historically based choices—the exodus, the gift of the land, the choice of the king, and the choice of Jerusalem. As never before, the theologians of ancient Israel had to consider how they could understand a god of history when all of the historical symbols of divine presence and sustenance were gone.

One means of understanding the disaster was to turn to Yahweh's actions in mythical time to portray a deity who stands outside of time, who in fact created time. Literature of the period draws upon cosmological myths such as the myth of Yahweh's battle in primordial time against the sea or sea monster (Ps. 74) and associates that event with the choice of the Davidic monarch (Ps. 89).[4] The psalmist does not reconcile the tension between the making and the unmaking of the Davidic covenant. Instead, he laments its loss while ending with the hope that Yahweh will remember the covenant with David and overturn the present humiliation of the king. In Psalm 102, the physical restoration of Zion is associated with the kingship of Yahweh *and* his role as creator: "Long ago you laid the foundation of the earth, and the heavens are the work of your hands. They will perish, but you endure" (102:25–26a). Myth and history come together in the liturgy of the exile to say that Yahweh is greater than history!

Although the liturgy of the templeless age is mournful, can we think of it as ultimately hopeful? Building on the form-critical work of Gunkel and the cult-contextual model of Mowinckel, Walter Brueggemann considers the final form of the lament genre within the setting of worship (1995). In his view, the very form of lament conveys meaning. The most basic elements of a lament include a description of the dire situation, a petition, and the belief in the certainty of being heard by the deity. The movement from disruption to resolution suggests that each painful prayer is actually a confession of trust in Yahweh's power and purpose to save. In this way, the lament form is ultimately hopeful. The use of poems of this type in worship suggests a fundamental belief in the willingness of Yahweh to incline his ear to hear and to be predisposed to act on behalf of the petitioner. The claim of all the psalms surveyed and even Lamentations is that Yahweh is king! The question raised in the liturgy, however, is whether Yahweh will choose to be king of this people again. That the people pray in the context of worship certainly suggests that they believe this to be true.

In addition, the final shape of the communal dirges of Lamentations indicates a future-oriented vision even when there are no explicit references to hope outside of the inserted wisdom section (Lam. 3:22–39). Tod Linafelt has shown that chapter 1 is laden with elements from the funeral dirge, but these lessen in chapter 2, and almost disappear in chapter 4 (2000b). The fifth and final chapter concludes Lamentations with a pure communal lament. The move from the use of the form and language of the dirge, with its death orientation, to the communal lament, with its embrace of life, suggests that in form, though not always expression, Lamentations turns toward hope.

---

4. For reasons to understand the creation motif in the Psalms historically as relating to the exodus alone, see Watson 2005.

In addition to describing the painful present, the laments make suggestions about the deity and about the human person as a means of rationalizing the disaster. Beyond enabling an understanding of the validity of complaint, the laments provide a variety of explanations and even wrestle with inexplicability by accusing the deity of heavy-handedness. The grief expressed wrestles with tragedy and moves beyond an orientation on the past toward a vision for the future. In worship, ancient Israel met, wept openly and unabashedly, quarreled with, accused, and praised, but in all remained committed to Yahweh with earnest hope in the miracle of divine intervention and restoration.

CHAPTER 3

The Aftermath of Disaster: II

Memory

I n the immediate aftermath of disaster, the literature of mourning provided a means to convey a variety of emotions. At the time historical
recital in what is known as the Deuteronomistic History also captured a
sense of loss by accounting for communal stories and shaping them into
a meaningful whole. Although at first glance the Deuteronomistic History appears to end on a depressing note, certain features of its historical
presentation beg the question of whether it conveyed a sense of a future
beyond disaster.

HISTORICAL RECITAL

The Deuteronomistic History (DtrH) is a term given to the historical
books of Joshua, Judges, First and Second Samuel, and First and Second
Kings, introduced by (part of) the book of Deuteronomy. Traditionally,
the books were treated in isolation from one another. After the successful application of Julius Wellhausen's source criticism[1] to the books of the
Pentateuch, scholars tried to locate J (Yahwist), E (Elohist), D (Deuteronomic), and P (Priestly) literary strands in the historical books. Although
largely unsuccessful, the study revealed a remarkable degree of overlap
with the book of Deuteronomy.

1. Source criticism is a method of interpretation that starts with a consideration of the literary material
that makes up the first five books of the Hebrew Bible. Wellhausen attributed to the Pentateuch four main
sources, classified according to the name of God employed by the writer and characteristic features. Source
criticism has come under increased scrutiny in recent years. For an overview, see Whybray 1995 and
Nicholson 1998.

Noticing the prominent Deuteronomic imprint on the historical books, Martin Noth argued persuasively in 1943 that a single author wrote Joshua to Kings as an independent historical work with the book of Deuteronomy as an introduction (ET 1981). What appeared to be the influence of Deuteronomy on the historical books was in fact the intentional work of an author whose acceptance of the Deuteronomic view of covenant led to his becoming known as the Deuteronomistic Historian. In Noth's view, the historian lived in Judah during the Neo-Babylonian period. His composition was apparently completed shortly after 562, because the story of the kingdoms concludes with the release of Jehoiachin from prison (2 Kgs. 25:27–30). According to Noth, the historian wrote his narrative with the aid of source documents and material such as the Deuteronomic law code of Deuteronomy 4:44–30:20; stories about Moses, conquest (Josh. 2–11), the judges (Judg. 3–12), and the ark; tales about Saul and David; and annals, lists, and prophetic legends. Thus a historian collected, ordered, selected, and theologically interpreted very different traditional materials and synthesized them into the story of ancient Israel.

In Noth's view, the purpose of the Deuteronomistic History was to justify the final downfall of the kingdom of Judah in 587, complete with the loss of the Davidic king and the destruction of the temple. The historian explained that Yahweh had no choice but to judge the people because they repeatedly failed to keep the covenant established on Mt. Horeb (D's equivalent of Mt. Sinai). For Noth, the message of the DtrH is wholly negative in that it highlights repeated infractions and ends with no hope for a future.

Noth situated the author of DtrH in Judah for two reasons. First, official and archival documents would have been more available in the homeland. Second, many of the oral traditions come from the region of Benjamin and Mizpah to the north of Jerusalem. The oral traditions reflect a Benjamin-centered viewpoint. In the book of Joshua, for example, the onslaught of the tribes proceeds from Benjamin. To Noth can be added two additional points in favor of a Judahite setting (Janssen 1956). First, Solomon's prayer in 1 Kings 8 portrays the temple not as a place of sacrifice, but as a place of prayer and intercession. Since sacrifices could not be made at a defiled site, the sanctuary as a place of prayer makes sense in the context of the sixth century. Second, it maintains a land-centered view with an emphasis on the destruction of the temple and concern for the people in Jerusalem rather than for those in exile.

Noth set the stage for further analysis of these books. The first major attempt to revise or refine Noth's hypothesis came from Frank Moore

Cross (1973). Since Cross's conclusions are followed by many, there is justification in speaking of a Cross school of interpretation (cf. Nelson 1981; Fretheim 1983). Cross recognized the validity of two points made by Noth. First, he agreed that there is a difference between Deuteronomy and the Tetrateuch (Genesis–Numbers). Second, he endorsed Noth's description of the Deuteronomist as a creative author and historian. In distinction to Noth, Cross noticed that the last four chapters of Kings differ perceptibly from the preceding ones, one significant point being the lack of a final closing speech like those isolated in key junctures of the history. Noth had argued that "at important points in the course of the history, Dtr. brings forward the leading personages with a speech, long or short, which looks forward and backward in an attempt to interpret the course of events, and draws the relevant practical conclusions about what people should do" (e.g., Josh. 1, 23, et al.) (1981: 5). The book of Kings ends without a message to the current generation. Second, Cross argued further that the prediction of the inevitability of punishment for the sins of Manasseh is of a different kind and is more generalized than the prophecy/ fulfillment structure of the earlier history. Finally, the prophets in the last sections are not named, nor are any specific events given.

In addition to the above, Cross also noticed that a good deal of the first part of the history, up until the last chapters, is thematically different. Thematically, the texts function to condemn the northern kingdom of Israel. In the main, the emphasis rests on the sins of Jeroboam, who constructed alternative Yahwistic shrines in the northern kingdom at Bethel and Dan. At the same time, the material stresses God's commitment to David and to the city of Jerusalem. Taken together, these features suggested to Cross that there was a previous edition of DtrH, compiled at the time of Josiah. Because it was during the reign of Josiah that a law book like Deuteronomy was found according to 2 Kings 22–23, it seemed likely, in Cross's view, that the first edition of DtrH functioned as ideological support for the reforms carried out by Josiah in response to the finding of the book of the law. DtrH asserted that the salvation of Judah results from David and his successor, Josiah, in order to buttress one of the main aims of the Josianic reform in the seventh century, the centralization of the cult in Jerusalem.

In the light of the failure of the promise to come to fruition, a second edition (Dtr2) explained the downfall of Judah and the early death of Josiah. The contention in the first edition (Dtr1) that Judah would not witness the same fate as her sister country Israel, because of David and pious Josiah, was proven by history to have been erroneous. After the fall of Jerusalem, a redactor sought to explain the downfall of Judah. Dtr2 showed that despite promises to David and all of Josiah's efforts to purify the cult, Judah fell as a result of the sins of Manasseh (2 Kgs. 21:2–15) (for a rather different portrait of Manasseh, see Stavrakopoulou 2004). The second historian completed the work of his predecessor and filtered its message by additions that can be isolated. If one accepts the double-redaction hypothesis of Cross, the first edition of DtrH would have been completed before the sixth century, when the historian had access to source materials. The real scarcity of details about what actually happened in Judah following the deportation of the exiles in 598 and the placement of the closing passage in Babylon, along with exhortations to pray towards Jerusalem in 1 Kings 8, suggest a Babylonian origin for the second edition.

Another type of reaction to Noth's hypothesis stems from the Göttingen school. Rudolf Smend (1971) argued for the appearance of redaction additions of legal material to the main history.[2] The main historical recital by the Deuteronomist is the basis to which at least two other blocks of material were added. One redactor is Deuteronomistic Nomistic (DtrN), whose main emphasis was the law. Another is Prophetic (DtrP), whose prophecies against the monarchy in Kings are fulfilled. The earliest historian (DtrH) supposedly produced his edition shortly after the rehabilitation of Jehoiachin around 560 BCE. The other two are later, but how much later remains a point of dispute. In a relatively recent monograph, Mark O'Brien shows how the insights afforded by the Cross and Göttingen schools can be joined (1989). Moving scholarship in another direction, Claus Westermann has argued that the material is too diverse to ascribe to a single author (1994).

At the moment, there is no consensus about how the material took shape; however, there is a discernible organization that warrants considering the material as a unity. If we accept Noth's general theory, even with the insights afforded by Cross and Smend, there are natural breaks within the history. Noth highlighted speeches from the Deuteronomic point of view at Joshua 1, 23; 1 Samuel 12; and 1 Kings 8, as well as authorical reflections in Joshua 12; Judges 2; and 2 Kings 17. To his list, Dennis McCarthy has added 2 Samuel 7 (1965). Some of the speeches can be used to divide the history into epochs: wilderness wanderings (ending with Moses' speech in Deut. 33, not included by Noth), infiltration west of the Jordan (Josh. 23),

---

2. Smend argued this point in an article. His ideas have been expanded and defended by his pupil Walter Dietrich (1972).

the period of the Judges (1 Sam. 12), the rise of the monarchy culminating in temple construction (1 Kgs. 8), and the decline of the monarchy concluding with the downfall of the kingdom. The more important themes of the work include an interest in the prophets, the covenant with David, receiving possession of the promised land as a gift from Yahweh, the importance of the law as a condition for Israel to maintain resident in Judah, the people's apostasy from Yahweh especially through their worship of other gods, and cumulative guilt, of both the people and their kings. DtrH appears to be a well-thought-out and organized document related specifically to the issue of the loss of the land. Its entire purpose is to explain the collapse of the kingdoms. In so doing, it recounts the history of Yahweh's saving deeds for his people, ancient Israel, and the nation's repeated lack of response to divine action and purpose. The division of the history into epochs provides an explanation for the tragedy by attributing the nation's downfall to recurring sin. In addition, DtrH carefully vindicates the actions of Yahweh in the events of 587. Yahweh is justified because in each period of its history ancient Israel violated its covenant agreement.

Through recital, DtrH rationalized the destruction of Judah. In particular, the historian answered the question of how a nation-state created and maintained by Yahweh could collapse so ignominiously. The premise of the history rests on regarding the law of Moses as binding on the people of ancient Israel. Mosaic law like that found in Deuteronomy 30:15–20 (cf. chap. 28) provided a measuring rod by which the society and monarchy of Judah were judged and found wanting. Besides serving as a measuring rod, proper observance of the law makes possible a long and blessed life in the land, with the inheritance of the promised land understood as Yahweh's gift to a population separated from the nations. Divine promises of life and death include these words:

> See, I have set before you today life and prosperity, death and adversity. If you obey the commandments of the LORD your God that I am commanding you today, by loving the LORD your God, walking in his ways, and observing his commandments, decrees, and ordinances, then you shall live and become numerous, and the LORD your God will bless you in the land that you are entering to possess. But if your heart turns away and you do not hear, but are led astray to bow down to other gods and serve them, I declare to you today that you shall perish; you shall not live long in the land that you are crossing the Jordan to enter and possess. (Deut. 30:15–18)

DtrH illustrates that after entry into the land the people consistently rebelled against the obligations established in the covenant with Yahweh by worshiping deities either in addition to or in distinction from Yahweh. To Judah, the fate of the northern kingdom of Israel served as an example of what would occur if Deuteronomic principles were not adopted. The history of the northern kingdom and the ascription of its downfall in 722 to the worship of other deities is rehearsed in 2 Kings 17. Inserted into the historical recital, Judah is likened twice to Israel as a word of warning and explanation: "Yet the Lord warned Israel and Judah by every prophet and every seer" (2 Kgs. 17:13a) and again, "Therefore the Lord was very angry with Israel and removed them out of his sight; none was left but the tribe of Judah alone. Judah also did not keep the commandments of the Lord their God but walked in the customs that Israel had introduced" (2 Kgs. 17:18–19). The historian carefully outlines how Judah followed in the ways of the northern kingdom by persisting in its worship of other deities. Because Judah is unable or unwilling to learn from the mistakes of its northern neighbor, it too will experience collapse.

DtrH implicates the entire society in disobeying the law and subjects even the Davidic king to its precepts. At David's installation as king, Yahweh's original promise to David through Nathan is an unconditional promise: "But I will not take my steadfast love from him, as I took it from Saul, whom I put away from before you. Your house and your kingdom shall be made sure forever before me; your throne shall be established forever" (2 Sam. 7:15–16). At a later point in the history of the nation, the conditions of Deuteronomy are imposed on the unconditional covenant with David. The success or failure of the kings rests on whether they observe the law. Before Solomon's succession, David warns his son:

> "Be strong, be courageous, and keep the charge of the Lord your God, walking in his ways and keeping his statutes, his commandments, his ordinances, and his testimonies, as it is written in the law of Moses, so that you may prosper in all that you do and wherever you turn. Then the Lord will establish his word that he spoke concerning me: 'If your heirs take heed to their way, to walk before me in faithfulness with all their heart and with all their soul, there shall not fail you a successor on the throne of Israel.'" (1 Kgs. 2:2–4)

After the collapse of Judah, one explanation for the disaster finds its expression in the merging of the Deuteronomic emphasis on the strict observance of the Sinai covenant and the Davidic covenant (see 1 Kgs.

8:25; 9:4–5; Deut. 17:18–19). Each monarch is judged on the basis of the law of Deuteronomy, especially on the demand for the proper worship of Yahweh as the sole deity in the sanctuary in Jerusalem. By this criterion, all the northern kings are condemned, as are all the southern kings except for Asa (1 Kgs. 15:11–14), Hezekiah (2 Kgs. 18:1–8), and Josiah (2 Kgs. 22–23). The worst king of them all was Manasseh, who is blamed for the fall of Judah (2 Kgs. 21:11–12; 23:26–27; 24:3–4). His sins provoked Yahweh's anger to such an extent that the deity rejected Judah. Even the cultic reforms of Hezekiah and Josiah failed to alter this verdict.

In addition to providing explanations for the downfall of Judah, DtrH reinterpreted traditions in order to justify how central features of the First Temple state could be destroyed. The reassessment of the Zion tradition of the temple provided another answer to the question of how the disaster could have happened. In Zion theology, as well as the choice of a king, the deity chose a place—the city of Jerusalem. In Jerusalem, the temple symbolized the location of the guiding and abiding presence of Yahweh among the people, with the ark of the covenant understood to represent the deity's throne in the innermost and most sacred part of the holy precincts. When Sennacherib's forces were turned back at the very gate of Jerusalem through miraculous circumstances in the eighth century BCE, the belief in the inviolability of Zion arose (Hayes 1963). The city of Yahweh could not fall to enemy invaders. In addition, the cult had been centralized in line with Deuteronomic principles. Nevertheless, the city and the temple fell. The inexplicable loss resulted in the reinterpretation of the temple as the earthly home of the deity.

The centralizing and purging of the sanctuary that took place in conjunction with Josiah's reforms aimed at limiting contact with unorthodox worship, particularly with foreign worship. Confining religious activity to the Jerusalem sanctuary was in part an effort to safeguard the purity of the cult. However, the intrusion of enemy forces and the destruction of the temple resulted in contact with impurity and its defilement. In order to safeguard the sanctity of the deity, Deuteronomic thinking reassessed traditions of Yahweh's presence (Clements 1965; Mettinger 1982). The temple was no longer considered the dwelling place of the deity. Instead, Yahweh's presence became more remote and the deity abode in the heavens. Concomitant with the insistence on the transcendence of Yahweh, the temple became the place where the deity's name dwelt (also known as Deuteronomic name theology) as exemplified in Solomon's prayer dedicating the temple:

"But will God indeed dwell on the earth? Even heaven and the highest heaven cannot contain you, much less this house that I have built! Regard your servant's prayer and his plea, O Lord my God, heeding the cry and the prayer that your servant prays to you today; that your eyes may be open night and day toward this house, the place of which you said, 'My name shall be there,' that you may heed the prayer that your servant prays toward this place. Hear the plea of your servant and of your people Israel when they pray toward this place; O hear in heaven your dwelling place; heed and forgive. (1 Kgs. 8:27–30; also 1 Kgs. 8:29; 14:21; 2 Kgs. 21:7; 23:27)

We saw earlier that the conditionalizing of the Davidic promise resulted in the blame for the disaster falling on Manasseh. After the tragic events of 587, there is a marked change in views about the temple and deity. In order to safeguard the holiness of Yahweh, views about the temple as the location of the indwelling presence of the deity change such that it becomes the location of a hypostasized manifestation of the divine presence—"the name of Yahweh."

DtrH recounted the history of ancient Israel since entry into the land of Canaan. It is clear that from that point the people rebelled against the principles of the covenant made with Yahweh in the wilderness. The history of ancient Israel was reassessed in the light of the collapse of Jerusalem. In particular, important traditions were evaluated anew to explain how Judah could fall.

THE CONTRIBUTION OF THE DEUTERONOMISTIC HISTORY

The history of the Deuteronomist(s) is certainly one that justified judgment and wrath, with few words of consolation. Does this document provide any vestige of hope? Noth saw the ending of the history as anything but hopeful, because it recounts cycles of recalcitrant behavior by the people and their monarchs that led to the downfall of the state and the loss of the land. Moreover, on the basis of the appearance of the phrase "as long as he lived" at the close of the history (2 Kgs. 25:30) he argued that Jehoiachin died in exile, thereby foreclosing on the possibility of a future Davidic king. The passage and the history itself thus close on a depressing note (see the review of scholarship in Murray 2001). If that were the case, one has to wonder why the history would have been written at all. Because Noth regarded the overarching theme as one of irreversible doom in that its purpose sought to justify the actions of God in destroying Israel, it comes as no surprise that scholars who succeeded him endeavored to locate more positive aspects in the literature.

Gerhard von Rad launched the first major argument against Noth's assessment of Dtr's purpose (but not his overall hypothesis). In his article on the theology of the Deuteronomic presentation (1966), von Rad focused on counterthemes that drew out promises for a future beyond disaster. In particular, he noted that the history consistently highlighted the importance of prophecy (cf. Dietrich's work on prophets). For the Deuteronomistic Historian, the deity's word mediated by the prophets always achieves fulfillment, for good or ill. For von Rad, the sure fruition of prophecy is a given. Through his careful study, he revealed that there is one prophecy that remains unfulfilled in the work, that is, the promise made to the Davidic house. In 2 Samuel 7, the prophet Nathan declares the Yahwistic promise that a Davidic king will always rule on the throne of Judah, no matter what. Since the king has been taken away and the relative independence of Judah destroyed, von Rad perceived that the promise to reinstate the Davidic king remains in the future.

In von Rad's view, the final reference to the release of King Jehoiachin from prison must be read in conjunction with the eternal promise to David. The ending of Kings is not as negative as Noth supposed, but rather points to the future possibility of the return of a ruling descendant of David. The hope for the restoration of the monarchy certainly appears in prophecy of this period, for example, Ezekiel, Haggai, and Zechariah 1–8. In recounting the history of the nation, the importance of prophecy as a countertheme in the material suggests that Yahweh's promises remain to be revealed at some future point.

Hans Walter Wolff (1975) launched the second major reappraisal of Noth's negative view of the history. In contrast to von Rad, Wolff finds a future orientation based not on promises, but on the role of repentance. He draws attention to the concept of repentance (literally from the Hebrew term *shub*, "to return"), which appears at key highpoints and in the great speeches of DtrH. Its appearance throughout demonstrates to Israel what the nation is required to do under the judgment of the exile: confess their guilt and return to the service of Yahweh, in order to create the foundation for a new relationship. The important role of repentance is expressed through Josiah, the one Davidic king to "return" to Yahweh (2 Kgs. 23:25). Josiah is the king who repents. The greatest king after David serves as a model for the community. Although Wolff stresses that the message includes only the people, not the monarchy, kings are not necessarily excluded from future promises, as the motif of repentance appears originally in a narrative about a king (note also the use of the term in conjunction with Solomon).

A third evaluation of DtrH has led to another positive view of its purpose. In a careful analysis of the text, Gerald Gerbrandt shows that one of the principles underlying the history is acceptance of the Deuteronomic understanding of the land (that covenant loyalty meant life in the land, disloyalty expulsion from the land) (1986). Given that one of the other key interests of DtrH is kingship, Gerbrandt shifts to concentrate his study on Hezekiah and Josiah, the two key figures who alone received completely positive evaluations. In general, the king can be thought of as a covenant administrator whose responsibility was to ensure continued existence in the land. All of the northern kings of Israel were judged to be evil according to the Deuteronomic standard; thus the kingdom fell in 722, and the people lost the land. The application of a Deuteronomic measuring rod to Judah reveals that six kings in the southern kingdom were judged to have been good in the deity's eyes, but they received only conditional praise. The history highlights two outstanding monarchs, Hezekiah and Josiah, as deserving of unconditional divine favor. Both exhibited covenant loyalty by reforming the cult along Deuteronomic lines. In addition, each provides a paradigm to emulate. Hezekiah is remarkable in that he is the king who trusts in Yahweh for the sure defense of Jerusalem. Josiah is distinguished, as Wolff has already pointed out, in that he turns to Yahweh in repentance. The focus of DtrH was Yahweh's chosen people Israel, but the central concept of the history has to do with the inheritance of the land. In order to facilitate Yahweh's promises, Gerbrandt finds that the monarch will mediate the covenant again. Based on this positive aspect of kingship, Gerbrandt understands the release of Jehoiachin in a positive way, along the lines of von Rad.

In addition to providing positive appraisals of the history, the analyses of von Rad, Wolff, and Gerbrandt shift the focus of the discussion away from the recalcitrant past actions of the people to the figure of the deity and Yahweh's role in the history. Following this insight, three things become clear:

> Throughout the Deuteronomistic History, Yahweh is shown to be in control of events.
> The history reveals a cyclical pattern of human/divine interaction: human disobedience resulted in divine wrath that led to human

repentance and then to divine mercy and forgiveness. The stories in the book of Judges exemplify the repetition of this
pattern. DtrH itself ends at the point of the execution of divine
judgment. Whether the release of Jehoiachin reveals divine favor
or a sad end to the history of a people, Kings ends without the
next stage in the cyclical pattern found elsewhere in the history.
The ambiguous ending stops the narrative at the point of punishment. Halted midcycle, the history encourages us, even urges
us, to fill in the gaps with what comes next. The people are to
repent and confess their sins, with the expectation that Yahweh
will again act on their behalf.

Yahweh acts consistently with the predictions of true prophets. What
is prophesied about the deity comes to pass. Even though promises made to David and the people are made conditional, the fact
remains that the fulfillment of unconditional promises looms.

Although many scholars have focused on the composition or theology
of DtrH, it is important to ascertain its function. How could this work
function after the collapse of Jerusalem? The cyclical nature of the history
suggests a liturgical recital. At least two of the laments surveyed in the
previous chapter contained historical retrospectives, and both included
confessions of sin. DtrH could function as a very long historical recital
with a similar aim and serve two purposes: (1) a didactic one, by teaching
history and ways to avoid repeating the mistakes of the past; and (2) a
liturgical one, by providing another means to worship Yahweh without
sacrifice. Wellhausen was surely correct when he spoke of DtrH as a confession. As a confession, DtrH is reminiscent of Lamentations, which suggests that when the people confess recalcitrant behavior, Yahweh will
forgive. The history ends awaiting Yahweh's response (much as the book
of Lamentations does). Hope for the future lies only implicitly within certain promises in the text itself; nevertheless, the Deuteronomistic History
holds forth the promise of a future because of the very nature of the deity.
The historian does not foresee how that future will come about or even
how it will take shape, but a future for the people of Judah is inevitable.

SUMMARY

At first glance, the liturgy and historiography written in the aftermath of
systemic collapse suggest despair and pessimism. But with closer analysis what appears hopeless actually evokes a future orientation. The

psalms (including Isa. 63:7–64:11) that responded to the collapse of Jerusalem in 587, the book of Lamentations, and the Deuteronomistic History grasp the sense of dismay and uncertainty that suffused the covenant people. In despair, overwhelmed by tragedy and suffering, ancient Israel grieved and turned to its deity with profound trust, holding on to a glimmer of hope for restoration. In his classic study of the psalms of praise and lament, Westermann raised concerns about the failure of modern society and communities of faith to value the grief-stricken (1981). The liturgy and history of this period attest the high regard in which thoughts of despair, sorrow, and disbelief were held. Rather than turning a blind eye to the human suffering that accompanied the fall of Jerusalem, the community brought tragedy into conversation with Yahweh. In recalling Yahweh's salvific actions in the creation of the cosmos and in their history as a people, they believed that their suffering mattered to the deity. Although the liturgy and history failed to celebrate restoration, they expressed a profound belief in Yahweh's ability to intercede in human affairs to save those burdened by tragedy.

The next chapter considers the prophecies of Jeremiah and Ezekiel, who predicted judgment and hope. Unlike the texts surveyed here, they had clear visions of both.

CHAPTER 4

Between Judgment and Hope

The literature of the templeless age captured communal grief and memory in liturgy and history. With both, the search for a hopeful message pointing to a restored future reveals only hints of reasons to believe in upcoming possibilities. However, it is rather different with the prophecies of Jeremiah and Ezekiel. Although both pronounced doom to the nation of Judah, they also offered reasons to believe in something beyond disaster. They are best categorized as prophets of woe and weal.

When prophets are mentioned with reference to the Hebrew Bible/ Old Testament, generally one thinks of those who have books named after them—known as the Classical Prophets or the Latter Prophets. These include Isaiah, Jeremiah, and Ezekiel, who are often grouped together with the twelve Minor Prophets (Hosea, Joel, Amos, Obadiah, Jonah, Micah, Nahum, Habakkuk, Zephaniah, Haggai, Zechariah, and Malachi; but excluding Daniel, who is included among the Writings in the Hebrew Bible). The Classical Prophets are distinguished from the Preclassical or Former Prophets in that oracles thought to stem from a prophetic figure—along with a variable degree of descriptive narrative about his life—appear in a collection given his name. The Former Prophets include anonymous figures like those found scattered in the early literature of ancient Israel (as in Num. 11:24–25, Judg. 6:7–10; 1 Sam. 10:10–13; 19:18–24; 1 Kgs. 13; 18:4; 2 Kgs. 17:13; 21:10; 23:21); leaders who took on prophetic roles, such as Moses, Aaron, Miriam, and Deborah; and the prophets who lived during the early monarchical period, such as Samuel, Nathan, Elijah, and Elisha. The early prophets tend to be known through narratives that describe their actions rather than by their words, although some of what they conveyed in speech is recorded. Another type of prophecy worthy of mention is apocalyptic, which is related in some respects to classical prophecy (Knibb 1982; Collins 1984; Hanson 1985; Cook 1995; Vanderkam 1998). In apocalyptic, the prophet has a vision of the end time (the eschaton), revealed through dreams and symbols. The book of Daniel is an example of this type of literature (as are chaps. 24–27 of Isaiah, called the Isaiah Apocalypse; the book of Joel; Zech. 9–14, esp. chaps. 12–14).

The understanding of the nature of prophecy in ancient Israel and the connection between the early prophets and the Classical Prophets has been informed by comparisons with similar figures in Egyptian, Mesopotamian, and Canaanite societies of the ancient Near East (Nissinen 2003) and anthropological studies (see Wilson 1980, 1987; Grabbe 1995). Prophets before the monarchy and before the death of Solomon appear to have been established figures in society, while those after the division of the kingdom delivered words of judgment to the king and the people from the periphery (although court prophets ratify the king's wishes during this time). According to the Deuteronomistic History, the kingdoms were destroyed because of a failure to respond to the warnings of the prophets (2 Kgs. 13–14; 21:10–15; 24:2).

The Classical Prophets appeared during the time of the Assyrian Empire in the eighth century BCE (Amos and Hosea prophesied to the northern kingdom of Israel while Isaiah and Micah prophesied to the southern kingdom of Judah). Later they foretold the downfall of the kingdom of Judah (Nahum, Habakkuk, Zephaniah), spoke through and after its collapse (Jeremiah, Ezekiel, Obadiah, Isa. 40–55, Haggai, Zech. 1–8), and continued exhorting the community and its leaders in the fifth century when Yehud fell under the imperial governance of the Persians (Isa. 56–66, Joel, Malachi, Zech. 9–14, and Jonah). Prophecy is thought to have changed in nature after the restoration of Yehud and would eventually cease. The templeless age is understood to be the critical juncture that marked the start of the so-called decline of prophecy (see Mason 1982, for an overview).

As a group, the Classical Prophets shared a function in society and formal characteristics. Their activities were located in history with formulae that gave their names and chronology. Their most basic function was to "steer Israel through great historical changes" (Wolff 1982: 16). In so doing, they spoke both to the community as a whole and to individuals. They were intermediaries who announced divine intentions. Their message can be broken into three themes. First, they spoke of the coming Day of Yahweh, which Amos defined as Yahweh's judgment on a nation that failed to keep its part of the covenant with ancient Israel's deity. Second, they regarded the divinely executed disaster as an opportunity for a new relationship with the deity; for example, Hosea spoke of correction and Isaiah of a remnant (Isa. 7:1–17; 28:16). Finally, they foresaw restoration and the possibility of a new relationship with Yahweh as, for example, in Jeremiah's new covenant (Jer. 31:31–34), Ezekiel's new heart and new spirit (Ezek. 11:19; 36:26–27), and Deutero-Isaiah's announcement of divine intervention extending even to non-Israelites (Isa. 49:6). The prophets spoke in a characteristic way, often introducing oracles with "Thus says Yahweh" (known as the divine messenger formula) and concluding with "Oracle or Utterance of Yahweh." The prophets also used stereotypical forms like diatribes, threats, and oracles of salvation to convey their message. History determined the veracity of the prophetic word, with true prophets mediating the words of the deity that came to fruition.

During the templeless age, when the leaders of ancient Israel sought to find meaning in the events that shook the kingdom of the Davidic covenant to its foundations, two prophets arose who provided an explanation for the disaster, as well as hope for a future beyond it. These figures are Jeremiah and Ezekiel. However, a more general prophetic response to the collapse of Jerusalem and Judah would also take place.

After the fall of Jerusalem, the prophetic collections that predated the period were edited and expanded. The extent of this redactional activity is debated, but the circles responsible have links with the Deuteronomic worldview. The clearest example of this type of work appears in the Deuteronomistic History, where the fate of the doomed nation is in part associated with the rejection of Yahweh's word foretold by the prophets. Deuteronomic principles are also applied in the book of Amos. Amos maintained a consistent focus on judgment for sin in his prophecies to the northern kingdom of Israel during the eighth century BCE. There may have been one or two redactions of his oracles after the fall of the northern kingdom in 722 BCE, when his words were transported to the southern kingdom (for a helpful introduction to this discussion, see Coote 1981, who simplifies the arguments made by Wolff 1977). A layer of tradition in Amos attributes the collapse of the northern kingdom to the failure to heed the prophetic word (for one example, see the analysis of Amos 7 in Williamson 1995). This thought parallels that of Deuteronomy and has led a growing number of scholars to speak of a Deuteronomic redaction of the prophetic literature taking place after the fall of

Judah (Römer 2000; Albertz 2003). It is clear that this type of editing occurred within the book of Jeremiah (Nicholson 1970; Thiel 1973).

Jeremiah and Ezekiel helped to steer a course for ancient Israel through and beyond destruction. In so doing, like the Deuteronomistic History, they functioned after the disaster as theodicy, by explaining the actions of Yahweh. We turn now to their oracles and the literature that bears their names. We will consider their oracles of judgment and hope and show points of correspondence and divergence. As the composition of both books requires further attention, an overview of each introduces the messages contained therein.

JEREMIAH

Jeremiah began his career as a prophet in the last years of the seventh century BCE when great world events were unfolding. Assyrian control over the ancient Near East began to wane and would eventually cease. According to the first verse of the book bearing his name, Jeremiah was born into a priestly family in the village of Anathoth, just north of Jerusalem. The opening of the book recounts the divine call and commissioning of the prophet (1:4–19). The narrative contains elements consistent with the call of other leaders and prophets in the Hebrew Bible: a statement of divine purpose, the reluctance of the prophet, divine reassurance, the commission, and the details of the message (the classic study of call narratives is that of Habel 1965). Yahweh appoints Jeremiah to be a prophet to the nations (vv. 9–10) and to announce destruction ("to pluck up and to pull down, to destroy and to overthrow"), but to indicate also a foundation for renewal ("to build and to plant"). Jeremiah's prophetic activity occurs during the reigns of the final kings of Judah—Josiah, Jehoiakim, Jehoiachin, and Zedekiah. According to the introduction, Jeremiah begins to prophesy in the thirteenth year of the reign of King Josiah, 626 BCE. The final verses of the book link the end of his activity with the release of King Jehoiachin from imprisonment in Babylon in 562. According to the two bookends, the prophecies of Jeremiah begin in Judah and end in Babylon, although according to the book the person Jeremiah was taken to Egypt.

The book divides into two halves along thematic and literary lines: chapters 1–25 contain poetry that presents the theme of unequivocal judgment, and chapters 26–52 contain prose narrative that turns to hopes for restoration.

Chapters	Coverage
1–25	Oracles predicting judgment on Judah and Jerusalem in poetry
26–36	Prose section providing hope for the future
37–45, 52	Recital of the fall of Jerusalem and its aftermath
46–51	Oracles against the nations (cf. 25:15–38)

Much of the poetry found in the first half of the collection is thought to stem from a historical Jeremiah, while the narrative of the second section is associated with the reception of his words by another audience. This general structure is not entirely accurate, however, because prose narrative and hope are interwoven in chapters 1–25, while poetry and judgment can be found in chapters 26–52. In the first half of the book, narrative material reminiscent of the language and the theological perspective of the Deuteronomistic History is interspersed among the oracles written in poetry. Moreover, a number of inconsistencies between the poetry and the prose are readily apparent. For example, the scathing attack of the prophet on the stubborn nature of the community in the oracles (6:10; 8:4–6; 13:23) is very different from the consistent appeal to the people to repent found in the prose literature (7:3; 18:7–11; cf. 26:3). The apparent lack of order and cohesion to the book led John Bright to declare it "a hopeless hodgepodge thrown together without any discernible principle of arrangement at all" (Bright 1965: lvi).

Since the foundational works of Bernard Duhm and Sigmund Mowinckel it has been common to attribute the material in the book of Jeremiah to three sources of tradition (Duhm 1901: x–xviii; Mowinckel 1914, 1946). Conventionally interpreters recognize within the book of Jeremiah three layers of material, often abbreviated A, B, and C. Category A (which can be taken to stand for "authentic") represents the poetic material, found mainly within chapters 1–25, that is thought to stem from the historical prophet Jeremiah. B, found mainly in chapters 26–45, refers to a type of biographical prose attributed to the authorship of Baruch, Jeremiah's scribe. It includes accounts written about Jeremiah and his activities from the perspective of a third-person eyewitness. Christopher Seitz has argued that this material stems from a scribal circle that remained in Judah after the fall of Jerusalem (1985; 1989b) and refers to it as the Scribal Chronicle. C (from the compiler of the book) is made up of prose sections that resemble the language and the literary style of Deuteronomy and the Deuteronomistic History, with concerns of particular interest to the community in exile in Babylon (Nicholson 1970, but see Thiel 1973, who places its composition in Judah).

Even though the book of Jeremiah has a difficult structure that is more interwoven than linear, it has a coherent message. The prophet declares judgment on Judah and presents reasons to believe in a future beyond destruction. The fact that others may have added to the message of the historical Jeremiah over time and in different circumstances attests to a deep respect for the prophet as a mediator of the divine word and for the timelessness of his words. The prophecies and the book will be considered according to what formed the basis of judgment and how hope was perceived beyond it.

Denouncing a Sinful Kingdom

The prophetic collection attributed to Jeremiah is extremely helpful in interpreting one response to disaster, as many of the prophecies stem from just after the destruction of the temple in 587 and date up to the time of the death of Gedaliah. In chapters 1–25, the message has a singular purpose: to explain the upcoming disaster as the judgment of Yahweh. According to Jeremiah 1–25, the people sinned by being faithless to the covenant to honor Yahweh alone and to establish social justice. In the book of Jeremiah judgment on the nation is expressed in two types of material: the oracles associated with the prophet himself and the prose additions to the book attributed to a later editor.

After receiving his call, Jeremiah condemns Judah and predicts the destruction of the nation. He draws on the language of judgment found in the prophets who preceded him. For example, like Hosea he compares the relationship between Yahweh and Judah to that between a husband and a wife; he says that Israel has shattered that relationship by spurning Yahweh and serving other gods (Jer. 2:33). He is also concerned with issues of communal interaction. In Jeremiah 5:1, he recounts Yahweh's search in vain for anyone practicing morality. One can see commonality with the social concerns of Amos and Hosea in Jeremiah's imagery of greed: "Scoundrels are found among my people. . . . Like fowlers they set a trap" (Jer. 5:26). In addition to concerns about social injustice, Jeremiah includes statements denouncing the worship of deities other than Yahweh. To a nation defined by a lack of moral and religious rectitude, the prophet uses vivid imagery to convey his message of impending doom. He visualizes the judgment to come in his examples of the loincloth (13:1–11), broken jar (19:1–13), and the visit to the potter's house

(18:1–11). Many of his oracles of woe exhibit the coming disaster in a type of prophetic activity called a sign-act, a physical action that conveys a message through symbolic actions. The oracles of Jeremiah are used sometimes as in 18:1–11 to exhort the people to change patterns of behavior before it is too late, but they are just as often simply declarative statements announcing doom and destruction. Jeremiah, like the prophets of the First Temple, understands that communal sin in the form of social injustice and improper religious practices brought about divine judgment.

Certain features of the book of Jeremiah suggest that it underwent editorial activity. There are, for example, headings applied to the prophecies (2:1–2; 7:1–2; 16:1; 27:1), the delineation of larger editorial units (chaps. 1–6; 18–20), doublets (8:10b-12//6:13–15; 46:27–28//30:10–11; 48:40b, 41b//49:22), added synchronisms (25:1; 32:1), and the addition of the name Jeremiah to oracles that would otherwise be anonymous (in chaps. 2–25). Instead of being random additions in a rolling manner by which oracles were continually updated in different time periods to meet new situations affecting the community (suggested by Carroll 1986 and Mc-Kane 1986), the editorial additions shape the material, clarify the speaker, and offer a theological interpretation. The final form establishes that "the book represents substantially the final literary expression and deposit of a tradition which grew and developed at the hands of a body of people who sought not only to transmit the prophet's sayings but to present an interpretation of his prophetic ministry and preaching on the basis of theological concerns and interests which were of vital importance for them in the age in which they lived" (Nicholson 1970: 4).

One of the clearest examples of the type of editorial activity that took place and its meaning is the insertion into the first half of the book of poetic portions of material called the confessions of Jeremiah (11:18–12:6; 15:10–21; 17:14–18; 18:18–23; 20:7–13) (O'Connor 1988). Although early studies concentrated on the confessions of Jeremiah in isolation from the book, it is now clear that these prophetic laments were placed purposefully in chapters 1–25 to convey meaning (Diamond 1987; O'Connor 1988; M. S. Smith 1990). So evocative of the personal distress of the prophet, the soliloquies of Jeremiah provide a consistent theological message of judgment in their immediate setting of chapters 11–20 and within the first half of the book. In so doing, they establish the authenticity of the prophet as the mediator of the divine word. In addition, they play a vital role in the overall scheme of the redactor; they clarify the radical nature of the accusations made against ancient Israel and attribute the disaster to punishment for sin. The location of the confessions shows that divine retribution is inevitable, because of the rejection of the prophet and repeated covenant violations (Diamond 1987; M. S. Smith 1990). As such, they illustrate reasons for the fall of the nation and function as theodicy.

The prose sermons of Jeremiah also convey meaning within the context of the first half of the book (Stulman 1998). The speeches, terminology, and conceptual ideas of Jeremiah's prose sermons are often similar to those forms found within Deuteronomy and the Deuteronomistic History (Janzen 1973: 20–21, 105–15; Nicholson 1970: 20–37; Stulman 1986). Within chapters 1–25 there are five large blocks of material, with four introduced by a prose sermon (2:1–6:30; 7:1–10:25; 11:1–17:27; 18:1–20:18; 21:1–24:10). Louis Stulman has shown that each macro unit portrays systematically the whittling away of the symbolic world and the social order of Judah (1998). Neither the temple nor the covenant nor the election of Israel as Yahweh's people nor the leaders of society can turn aside the indictment against Judah and Jerusalem introduced in the first macro unit (cf. McConville 1993). Rather than being exhortation, the prophecies against the people and the kings are revelation. As such, they testify to the closing down of the possibility of repentance and the irrevocable nature of the divine response perceived in terms of an exile. At the same time, they contain hints that after the disaster a future may be possible for a segment of the population.

Through the application of the prose sermons of Jeremiah to the oracles, the original message of the prophet has been subsumed under a more general rubric that unifies the first half of the book. As Stulman has shown, the prose narrative portrays the community's interaction with the prophet Jeremiah as a mirror for the events that unfold. The rejection of Jeremiah validates impending and unequivocal judgment while at the same time his acceptance suggests the possibility of survival.

The message of destruction is conveyed partly through the association of Jeremiah and Moses. The prose narrative portrays Jeremiah as a prophetic successor to Moses, who was regarded as the prophet par excellence in Deuteronomic ideology. As such, the prophet serves as a figurehead for the totality of the disaster (Mowinckel 1914: 38; Holladay 1989: 62; Seitz 1989a). Although Moses and Jeremiah intercede for the people, Yahweh in the book of Jeremiah forbids the prophet to continue to act in this role (7:16; 11:14; 14:11; 15:1) (Seitz 1989a). Interspersed among the prophecies of chapters 11–20, the prose sermons of Jeremiah illustrated the necessity for the collapse of every social, political, and religious system by foreclosing on the inheritance of the land, the monarchy, and even prophecy. The portrait of Jeremiah as a Mosaic figure reinforces the presentation of societal collapse.

Jeremiah's announcement of judgment on unfaithful members of society does not cease after the fall of Jerusalem. To the prophet are attributed words of judgment for the community remaining in Judah under the leadership of Gedaliah (Jer. 24). In addition, after the text placed Jeremiah in Egypt (Jer. 43:6–7), the prophet is said to have condemned the population that sought refuge there. In Jeremiah 44, his attack on the people is particularly scathing. Because they continue the unorthodox worship practices that brought about Yahweh's wrath in the first place, they will be eradicated. In the latter part of the collection, every community except the one that experienced deportation to Babylon falls under judgment. The final redaction of Jeremiah (the C material) denies the possibility of a future for any group but the *golah.*

In the book of Jeremiah the message of the prophet turns increasingly to the irrevocability of judgment on a people who have sinned for breaking the conditions of the Yahwistic covenant and for rejecting the prophetic messenger of the divine word. The complete destruction of past systems symbolic of Yahweh's relationship with Judah, including the political, religious, and social authorities, were announced through oracles, confessions, and prose sermons.

Future Possibilities

The first half of the book functions to show the necessity of divine judgment, but McConville has shown that the narrative material provides hints of renewal (1993). Hope for the community in the early chapters rests with those exiled to Babylon (cf. 16:14–16; 23:5–6). The focus on salvation made possible through the deported population certainly suggests that the words of Jeremiah were redacted in Babylon to provide hope to the exiles (Nicholson 1970; McConville 1993; Stulman 1998). Although Janzen argues that the setting of the editorial work on Jeremiah should be traced to the use of the prophetic oracles in sermons to edify those who remained behind in Judah, it is difficult to see how this would transpire in a meaningful way. The *Tendenz* of the material in chapters 1–25 clearly demonstrates that the possibility of redemption requires judgment in the form of a complete break with the social structures of the past. Because of the stubbornness of the people and their inability to perceive the truth, all facets of Judahite life, including every sign of the covenantal relationship between Yahweh and the people—the temple, the land, and the monarchy—will be subject to divine vengeance. It would hardly be any consolation to the Judahite population that remained in the land after 587 that the future of the people and the nation rests solely with their exiled brethren. These hints of hope directed to the Babylonian exiles beg the question of for whom the prophet (or better, the prophetic book) foresaw restoration.

Even though it is unclear whether the historical Jeremiah ever held out hope beyond the disaster of the fall of Jerusalem, there is a significant amount of hope in the book directed to different groups—to Judah, to the exiles, to individuals, and to the king. In the book of Jeremiah, it is clear that there is a time limit of seventy years on God's punishment: "Then after seventy years are completed, I will punish the king of Babylon and that nation, the land of the Chaldeans, for their iniquity, says the LORD, making the land an everlasting waste" (Jer. 25:12) and "For thus says the LORD: Only when Babylon's seventy years are completed will I visit you, and I will fulfill to you my promise and bring you back to this place" (Jer. 29:10). Babylon executed the judgment predicted by the classical prophets such as Amos, Hosea, Nahum, Habakkuk, and, indeed, Jeremiah, but God's anger does not hold sway forever. For the most part, scholars have concentrated attention on the hopeful message in the C material that is directed to the community in Babylon. In recent years, renewed interest in assessing the situation of the homeland has led to an examination of prophecies of salvation directed to the population in Judah following the collapse of Jerusalem, found in the B material. A consideration of Jeremiah's hope will cover both addressees of the prophet's message—those in Judah and those in Babylon.

Hope for Judah

A number of prophecies in the B material attributed to Baruch or, more appropriately, the scribal chronicle hold out hope for the community that remained in Judah following the events of 598 and 587 and the death of Gedaliah. Eventually, the prophecies of Jeremiah would be transferred to Babylon, where the message would serve to sustain the exiles in their context.

A series of Jeremianic prophecies suggests that submission to Yahweh would result in life and blessing in the land of Judah (Jer. 27:8–11; 38:17–20). These prophetic predictions of divine good will were conditional on the nation's response and were not fulfilled. Even so, prophetic rhetoric continued to emphasize divine intentions for a positive future for those in the homeland. After the fall of Jerusalem, Jeremiah sets an example for the people when he chooses to remain in Judah, even though the commander of the army offered the opportunity to go to

Babylon (Jer. 40:4–6). As a prophet, Jeremiah represented Yahweh's ongoing presence with and purposes for the people (see Lipschits 2005, for more on positive Jeremianic oracles to the homeland).

In addition to the prophetic words and actions that indicated divine purposes for the well-being of the community in Judah, the appointment of Gedaliah fostered a sense of stability. His leadership promised a future beyond disaster, and Gedaliah himself addressed the community left behind in the land. Gedaliah encouraged the remnant as well as refugees who had fled to neighboring countries to inhabit Judah and accept Babylonian rule (Jer. 40:9–12). After Gedaliah's assassination, Jeremiah again assumes a role of leadership and guidance for the people by advising the royalists who murdered Gedaliah to submit to Babylonian rule (Jer. 42:7–43:7). With words echoing his call, he proclaims, "Thus says the LORD, the God of Israel, to whom you sent me to present your plea before him: If you will only remain in this land, then I will build you up and not pull you down; I will plant you, and not pluck you up; for I am sorry for the disaster that I have brought upon you" (42:9–10). Even in the face of continued disobedience to the word of the deity, Jeremiah holds out hope for the community in Judah who survived the series of Babylonian attacks.

In a few scattered verses, Jeremianic prophecies predict a blessed future in the land for those who remained. At least one of the predictions of blessing was fulfilled. Seitz has drawn attention to a brief statement made in the Gedaliah account that shows divine blessing on the people in the land (1985; 1989b). After Gedaliah's speech urging everyone to remain in the land of Judah, an editor relates that "then all the Judahites returned from all the places to which they had been scattered and came to the land of Judah, to Gedaliah at Mizpah; and they gathered wine and summer fruits in great abundance" (Jer. 40:12). The description of the abundance of the harvest indicates Yahweh's blessing on those in the land.

Hope for Paradigmatic Individuals

Although certain phrases in the scribal account of Jeremiah indicate that restoration occurred among the population that remained in Judah, the prophetic message has been shaped to demonstrate that the Judahites constantly rejected the divine word. The prophecies in the book, therefore, shift their focus to individuals who hear and respond positively to Jeremiah, as a means to hold out hope for a different community.

The second half of the book, chapters 26–52, is set in the aftermath of 587. It explains the disaster further, but turns to divine promises of a future to the community in exile. Like the oracles in chapters 1–25, the prose narrative is organized by editors. In particular, it appears that framing passages have been established to highlight its main themes. These framing passages, chapters 26, 36, 45, and 52, draw a contrast between those who heed Jeremiah and those who do not, with most focusing on the former by portraying the positive reception of the prophet's message. The second half of the book is bounded by a summary of Jeremiah's temple sermon in chapter 26 (cf. chap. 7) and a reiteration of the destruction of Jerusalem in chapter 52. In between, two important chapters demarcate the material further: chapter 36 vividly portrays the reasons for the rejection of the succession of the Davidic line, and chapter 45 provides the transfer of prophetic authority to Baruch. Each of these units explains the disaster further and indicates a positive future beyond it.

The insertion of an abbreviated form of the temple sermon in chapter 26 correlates the failure of the people to obey Yahweh with the ruination of the symbols of divine presence, that is, the temple and Jerusalem. The prose introduction highlights the general dismissal of Jeremiah's message by the people as well as civic and religious leaders. However, the section is not completely pessimistic. An interesting contrast is made between the rejection of Jeremiah and his acceptance. For the first time in the book, recorded at the beginning of the prose narrative, a faithful remnant perceives Jeremiah as a true prophet (O'Connor 1989). They heed the prophet's message:

> Then the officials and all the people said to the priests and the prophets, "This man does not deserve the sentence of death, for he has spoken to us in the name of the Lord our God." And some of the elders of the land arose and said to all the assembled people, "Micah of Moresheth, who prophesied during the days of King Hezekiah of Judah, said to all the people of Judah: 'Thus says the Lord of hosts,
>
>> Zion shall be plowed as a field;
>> Jerusalem shall become a heap of ruins,
>> and the mountain of the house a wooded height.'
>
> Did King Hezekiah of Judah and all Judah actually put him to death? Did he not fear the Lord and entreat the favor of the Lord, and did not the Lord change his mind about the disaster that he had pronounced against them? But we are about to bring great disaster on ourselves!" (Jer. 26:16–19)

The sudden appearance of a group that accepts Jeremiah and argues for his validity opens up the possibility of hope for a select few after the disaster. The final section of the book deals specifically with the remnant who avidly received the prophetic word. The conception of hope with reference to the *golah* strongly suggests that they are that group.

The next two narrative introductions, at chapters 36 and 45, continue the theme of the rejection and acceptance of Jeremiah. Chapter 36 demonstrates the king's rejection of Jeremiah by petulantly cutting up the scroll on which his prophecies were written and throwing it into the fire. In response, Jeremiah says that in contrast to the word of Yahweh, which will endure and be rewritten, the reign of Jehoiakim will pass away. In another framing narrative, the image of the fate of the nation intertwines with the possibility of hope resting in people who hear Jeremiah, accept his message, and follow his teaching. In a touching passage in chapter 45, Jeremiah directs a prophecy to Baruch, his pupil and scribe. In this short chapter of only five verses, Jeremiah contrasts the eradication of the nation and "all life" to the blessed life of his protegé. Again, the message in the framing chapters of the book highlights future possibilities for those who heed the divine word and the divine messenger.

Chapter 52 provides a fitting conclusion to the entire literary collection of Jeremiah's oracles. Many think of it as an epilogue. In it the editor juxtaposes the main themes of the two halves of the book, disaster and promise. In the first place, it shows how Jeremiah's oracles of doom were confirmed in the events of 587. After a lengthy reiteration of the destruction of the city and deportation, the author depicts a scene in Babylon. The future restoration of the nation under a Davidic king is a distinct possibility, because the book closes with the release of King Jehoiachin from prison:

> In the thirty-seventh year of the exile of King Jehoiachin of Judah, in the twelfth month, on the twenty-fifth day of the month, King Evil-merodach of Babylon, in the year he began to reign, showed favor to King Jehoiachin of Judah and brought him out of prison. (Jer. 52:31)

In addition, the parable of the wicked and good shepherd appeared in an earlier text that illustrated the restoration of the Davidic line. Therein the restored monarch performed the role of the good shepherd (Jer. 23) and becomes in Jeremiah another type of individual destined for renewal.

Although the second half of the book confirms the need for the absolute and ultimate judgment of Judah, it also holds out the possibility of hope for a select and chosen few. Future salvation lies with those to whom the prophetic mantle has been passed. The Babylonian exiles received the oracles of Jeremiah and reinterpreted them. The message of Yahweh mediated through Jeremiah continued to provide succor for them in a far distant land.

Hope for the Exiles

Especially in the C material—the prophecies of Jeremiah that are updated to speak directly to the *golah* in Babylon—his message shifts to the exiles alone. An example of the transfer is in the parable of the good and the bad figs:

> And the LORD said to me, "What do you see, Jeremiah?" I said, "Figs, the good figs very good, and the bad figs very bad, so bad that they cannot be eaten." Then the word of the LORD came to me: Thus says the LORD, the God of Israel: Like these good figs, so I will regard as good the exiles from Judah, whom I have sent away from this place to the land of the Chaldeans. I will set my eyes upon them for good, and I will bring them back to this land. I will build them up, and not tear them down; I will plant them, and not pluck them up. . . . But thus says the LORD: Like the bad figs that are so bad they cannot be eaten, so will I treat King Zedekiah of Judah, his officials, the remnant of Jerusalem who remain in this land, and those who live in the land of Egypt. (Jer. 24:3–6, 8)

According to the prophecy, only the community that experienced the judgment of exile had the possibility of a future. The book of Jeremiah has been shaped to show that every facet of life had to be transformed. Since the people who remained in the land after the fall of Jerusalem and the people who fled to Egypt were not thought to have experienced Yahweh's wrath fully, the editors predicted more destruction for them.

The C material of Jeremiah clarifies the recipients of Yahweh's promises with particular poignancy for the Babylonian exiles, to whom a return like the exodus was predicted. Furthermore, the escalating prediction of doom in the first half of the book illustrated the need for the complete execution of Yahweh's judgment. Through the lenses of the Deuteronomic editors it became clear that the only possibility for future hope lay in a new exodus made possible by the return of the exiles from Babylon.

This section considers more carefully two of the passages of hope. One of the clearest promises made to the exiles is found in Jeremiah 29, in what is known as Jeremiah's letter to the exiles. The letter assures them that their sojourn will be a long one and urges them to settle in Babylon: to build houses and live in them, to plant gardens and eat their produce, and to marry and have children. After a length of time in accordance with divine intention, Jeremiah relates Yahweh's promises to gather them together and deliver them (Jer. 29:10–14).

The second passage is one of the most extraordinary in the whole book. It could be understood to provide hope to all people, because it focuses on divine rather than human initiative. According to Jeremiah's predictions of doom, everything had to be utterly destroyed because of corruption. This ideology holds true for the covenant between Yahweh and the people as well. However, because Yahweh's word stands and remains true for all time and Yahweh could not reject the covenant completely, the prophet proclaims the establishment of a new covenant. The description of the new covenant occurs in chapters 30–31, a section of material found in the Booklet of Consolation (chaps. 30–33):

> The days are surely coming, says the LORD, when I will make a new covenant with the house of Israel and the house of Judah. It will not be like the covenant that I made with their ancestors when I took them by the hand to bring them out of the land of Egypt—a covenant that they broke, though I was their husband, says the LORD. But this is the covenant that I will make with the house of Israel after those days, says LORD: I will put my law within them, and I will write it on their hearts; and I will be their god, and they shall be my people. No longer shall they teach one another, or say to each other, "Know the LORD," for they shall all know me, from the least of them to the greatest, says the LORD; for I will forgive their iniquity, and remember their sin no more. (Jer. 31:31–34)

Here the editors speak of the new covenant in association with the old one made during the flight from Egypt. After the first exodus, the covenant was broken. Whereas the old covenant was made of tablets of stone, the new covenant will be written upon human hearts. Although the material on which Yahweh confirms divine commitment to the people is different, the promise remains the same. Yahweh is the God of the people of Judah, and they shall be Yahweh's people. Only the means of accessing the covenant is changed. A relationship with the deity is made possible through a renewal of the heart, mediated to each person individually. Jeremiah's new covenant makes available an intimate, personal relationship with Yahweh: "They shall all know me, from the least of them to the greatest."

The book of Jeremiah alternates between messages of destruction and renewal. Although the prophecies of judgment are comprehensive and wide ranging in their magnitude, salvation oracles promise a future beyond disaster. Initially inclusive, the recipient of the salvific promises is narrowed to a select portion of the community that inherits the words of the prophet and interprets them anew. A new covenant, offered to a restored community, will ensure an ongoing relationship between the deity and the people.

EZEKIEL

Ezekiel was a contemporary of Jeremiah. Up until the first Neo-Babylonian incursion in 598 BCE, Ezekiel lived in Jerusalem. At that time, he was exiled with Jehoiachin. According to the chronological framework of the book, Ezekiel's ministry lasts from 592/1 (1:2–3) to 571/0 (29:17),[1] up to and just following the destruction of Jerusalem. Before the disaster Ezekiel spoke to the exiles about the approaching judgment on the city of Jerusalem. After that horrific event, he concentrated on hope for future renewal and restoration in a series of proclamations and visions.

Walter Zimmerli's observation about Ezekiel affects how we understand his prophetic activity:

> Despite the many features that Ezekiel has in common with Jeremiah, this prophet . . . is a fundamentally different figure. He exhibits none of Jeremiah's agitated suffering. According to 3:9, Yahweh makes his brow "like adamant, harder than flint." This is also the nature of Ezekiel's message. He has none of Jeremiah's powerful eloquence, none of the human emotion that seems to make Jeremiah so much more directly accessible. Instead, this prophet with his priestly background has a special sense that Yahweh . . . is in the process of revealing himself not just to this people, but to the entire world of the nations. (Zimmerli 1978: 207)

---

1. In the literature on Ezekiel, the dates vary among interpreters by one year. This is due to the fact that two types of dating schemes are employed in the Hebrew Bible. The first reflects an older Hebrew custom of dating the months of the year from autumn to autumn. The second corresponds to the Neo-Babylonian custom of dating from spring to spring. Jeremiah and 2 Kings number their dates according to the Babylonian system. There is some disagreement over which system Ezekiel used.

As Zimmerli has remarked, the prophet Ezekiel differs from Jeremiah in significant ways. In fact, the book that bears Ezekiel's name, unlike the book of Jeremiah and most the other prophets, is more literary than oracular in character. In the other prophetic books, the focus lies on the spoken word, and formulae distinguish speeches from narrative. In addition, addresses of the other prophets thought to be typical of ancient Israelite prophecy—like those of diatribe or threat—do not appear. Instead Ezekiel's prophetic message is conveyed through lengthy, well-thought-out literary compositions more akin to essays or discourses (e.g., chaps. 16, 18, 20, 23). Although Ezekiel is included among the prophets, his ministry is markedly literary in character. Another feature that distinguishes Ezekiel from other prophetic books such as Isaiah or Jeremiah is the sophisticated and systematic dating scheme applied to the prophetic activity.

One can think of a prophetic spectrum, in which Ezekiel is like the other prophets in some respects, but unlike them in others. In the first place, Ezekiel is distinguished as being a priest or of a priestly line (1:2–3). Unlike the writings of Jeremiah—whose father was also a priest—much of the language used in Ezekiel is like that used by priests (such as the legal injunctions in Ezek. 18:5–18). Furthermore, he shows a great deal of concern with cultic matters, especially the regulation of religious ritual, both orthodox and unorthodox. The clearest example of his focus on improper worship appears in the (in)famous temple vision in which he is shown illicit cultic practices taking place around and within the sanctuary (chaps. 8–11). Otherwise, the prophet speaks frequently against the worship of other deities. The focus on cultic matters remains sustained through the concluding chapters that contain the prophet's vision of the purified temple (chaps. 40–48). The distinctive character of the book as written prophecy with the terminology and concerns of the priesthood has resulted in speculation that Ezekiel was a priestly intruder into the prophetic line. The fact that Hosea also commented to a large extent on worship practices, however, should caution against too great a divide between the prophets and the priesthood.

The book of Ezekiel itself can be divided into two main sections based on thematic concerns. The first section, chapters 1–24, concerns the approaching fall of Jerusalem and the dissolution of the state. The second section, chapters 25–48, concentrates on a central theme: the restoration of Jerusalem and the reconstitution of the state as a religious community. The book divides into four sections based on literary divisions:

Chapters	Coverage
1–24	The approaching fall of Jerusalem and the dissolution of the state, addressed to the Judahite population and to Jerusalem
25–32	Oracles against the nations
33–39	Promises of hope and restoration, addressed to the exiles
40–48	Specific promises of hope directed to a community returned to Jerusalem with concerns about the temple, its reconstruction, regulations for its personnel, and its place in the restored community

The composition of the book of Ezekiel has long been discussed. Josephus reported already in the first century CE that Ezekiel left two books. In the eighteenth century, Josephus's reference to two books came to be associated with chapters 1–39 and 40–48, with the latter taken to be spurious. Ever since that time, there has been a long history of debate about the literary integrity of Ezekiel.

The traditional view understands Ezekiel to be the author of the whole book (a representative is Greenberg 1983). One of the more obvious reasons for this has to do with the homogeneity of the collection. In both its theological outlook and literary structure, the book of Ezekiel corresponds well to a unified composition. The prophecies move from themes of judgment and doom in the first half of the collection to themes of salvation and restoration in the second half. Its literary character and the systematic progression of the dating formulae contribute to arguments in favor of a single author. Similarly, the repetition of key phrases contributes to a sense of overall unity.

Although the prophecies of Ezekiel at first glance appear to be a unified composition by a single author, there are several indications that the situation might be otherwise. As with the book of Jeremiah, the appearance of a systematic chronology provides some indication that there was a purpose behind the arrangement of the book. The numerical sequence is out of order in three places. Interestingly, it is broken only in the section in which the oracles against the nations appear. There is general agreement that the oracles against the nations were grouped according to theme rather than time frame. Another indication of editorial activity is the dual superscription that introduces the book. Ezekiel opens with two headings that relate to an aspect of his prophetic ministry. The first, at 1:1, recounts the experience of the call from a first-person perspective:

"In the thirtieth year, in the fourth month on the fifth day of the month, as I was among the exiles by the river Chebar, the heavens were opened." The second recounts the call from the point of view of a third person (an eyewitness or a narrator): "On the fifth day of the month (it was the fifth year of the exile of King Jehoiachin), the word of the LORD came to the priest Ezekiel" (1:2–3). Differences between the headings likely indicate that they stem from different sources. In addition, they reflect two different dating schemes. The first verse speaks of an ambiguous thirtieth year, which could refer to the age of the prophet or some other referent, while the second passage delineates time according to the period of the deportation of King Jehoiachin. Another feature suggestive of different sources for the headings is the shift in person.

These two factors together—the ordering of the oracles against the nations according to themes, and the appearance of editorial comments—suggest that the book in its present form may stem from a redactor. A further argument in favor of a redactor is that judgments of complete and utter destruction found in the first half of the collection are tempered with prophecies of hope. At the end of passages about the totality of destruction are verses that provide a sense of future beyond disaster. The sudden appearance of words of salvation in passages of doom suggests that additions were made to Ezekiel's prophecies. An example occurs in chapter 16, where Ezekiel tells the story of the city of Jerusalem personified. Abandoned as an infant, the deity rescued and adopted Jerusalem. After she grew to sexual maturity, Yahweh married her and provided her with beautiful clothes and fine food. But Jerusalem betrayed her husband, making idols, sacrificing human beings and children to idols, and liaising with foreign nations like Assyria, Babylon, and Egypt. In response, Yahweh declares that her lovers will gather as a mob to stone her, cut her to pieces, and burn her houses to the ground. A word of hope (vv. 42–43) interrupts the violent allegory and the passage concludes with words of salvation (vv. 53–63). The concluding message appears odd, given the intent of the allegory to illustrate divine judgment on the city. Moreover, passages of restoration fit better with the oracles of salvation in the second half of the book. The insertion of positive passages in the midst of language of overriding judgment suggests editorial activity.

These features indicate that a later hand redacted the prophetic book of Ezekiel. Based on evidence for redaction, Zimmerli (1979) argued that a school of thought edited Ezekiel's prophecies. Refining his argument, Ronald Clements associated the redactor with the school responsible for the Holiness Code in Leviticus 17–26 and the Priestly work in the Tetrateuch (1982). In Clements's view the editor probably completed his redaction around 538, at the time of the rise of the Persian Empire, but certainly no later than 516 (1982). Systematic dating formulae and cultic concerns were of particular relevance to the Priestly writers. The unified focus on the temple and its centrality to the restored community in the final chapters of the book (chaps. 40–48) has long been thought to be an addition. The concerns therein with the role and sanctity of the priesthood provide additional support for Clements's identification of the final redaction of Ezekiel with the Priestly writers. Although the book of Ezekiel bears a unity of theme and purpose that allows an analysis of its final form, the final chapters will be treated in the next chapter, as they functioned along with Deutero-Isaiah to clarify a future beyond disaster. Nevertheless, Ezekiel's message fits well with prophecy of judgment and hope.

Irreversible Doom

Like Jeremiah, Ezekiel offers a message of advancing judgment. Unlike Jeremiah, Ezekiel never offers the possibility of repentance to avoid disaster. Instead, Ezekiel is termed a "sentinel" (Ezek. 3:17; 33:2), that is, one who stands at the ramparts of a city and warns inhabitants of approaching armies. Like a sentinel, the prophet announces the finality and totality of imminent disaster, rather than calling for repentance. The fact that Ezekiel prophesies among the exiles in Babylon also conveys the irrevocability of judgment. His words are not meant to address the community in Judah; rather, they are intended to explain the situation in the homeland to people at a distance who are anxious about their homes and relatives. There is no possibility of repentance on behalf of those left behind to assuage the anger of the deity.

Like other prophets commissioned by Yahweh, Ezekiel is called to perform a specific task (1:1–3:15). It is helpful to compare the commissioning of Ezekiel with that of Isaiah, because both men had visions of the deity on a throne. In distinction to Isaiah's call and commissioning, in which Isaiah claims that he saw Yahweh (Isa. 6), Ezekiel makes it clear through constant allegory and comparison that he only sees a likeness of the deity. By so doing, he conveys a sense of the incomparability of Yahweh. Secondly, Isaiah saw Yahweh and his presence in the Jerusalem temple. In Ezekiel's vision, the likeness of the deity comes to Ezekiel in Babylon. The very first chapters of Ezekiel emphasize the mobility of Yahweh, particularly the availability of the divine presence to the exiles in Babylon. The wheels on the deity's chariot in the vision reveal that Yahweh is not tied to a specific place (Kutsko 2000; Klein 2002).

The deity has the freedom to move away from the defilement brought about by the people's violations of the covenant. A holy God cannot exist among an impure people. Through the call narrative Ezekiel is shown to be a prophet who announces rather than exhorts. There is no possibility for change and repentance, no way to forestall disaster. The people are doomed (see Ezek. 2:3–7). Whether or not they choose to hear, the onus of Ezekiel's burden is to deliver the message. Furthermore, he accepts the commissioning by eating a scroll that is offered to him. The exact words of the scroll are not revealed, but its content is clear. On the scroll were written, "words of lamentation and mourning and woe" (2:10). The message Ezekiel is called to impart is not to be a pleasant one. He foreshadows doom and destruction. Indeed, he foretells the coming "day of the Lord" or the time of Yahweh's judgment of his people predicted by the former prophets. Ezekiel the priest becomes a prophet of doom.

In the course of his message, Ezekiel performs sign-acts where he acts out the coming disaster for his contemporaries in exile. All the symbolic actions of Ezekiel except one (Ezek. 37:15–28) function visually to represent the disaster about to overtake Jerusalem. Here are few examples:

4:1–3	Ezekiel deploys mud bricks to provide a visual representation of the siege,
4:9–17	bakes unclean bread and eats it to portray siege conditions,
5:1–4	cuts his hair to symbolize the fate of the nation: a third of the population will be slaughtered, a third will die of disease, and a third will go into exile, and
12:1–11	carries baggage to show that many Judahites will be refugees.

Each of the sign-acts in the first part of the book, placed literarily before the announcement of the destruction of Jerusalem, illustrates the devastating effects of Yahweh's coming judgment. Interestingly, the symbolic actions function as a report to the population in Babylon. As such, their inclusion confirms the association of Ezekiel with a sentinel. Ezekiel acts out situations to his audience in Babylon to show them visually what suffering will be like in Jerusalem and Judah. In a world without television, Ezekiel's sign-acts portrayed a living disaster.

Ezekiel also experienced visions in which he is transported to Jerusalem to see the sinful things taking place there. The most dramatic example of the need for judgment on Jerusalem occurs in what could be thought of as the abominable temple vision in chapters 8–11. In chapter

8 a heavenly messenger transports Ezekiel from Babylon to Jerusalem, where the spirit shows him four scenes of various people worshiping deities other than Yahweh. According to the spirit each act is more abominable than the last. The worship of other deities in the temple complex provides visual confirmation of the sanctuary's defilement and thereby explains the judgment that is to come. The inevitability of disaster is confirmed by the death of Pelatiah, who represents the wicked inhabitants of Jerusalem (11:13) and by the fact that the presence of Yahweh travels up from the Holy of Holies in the temple to hover on the outskirts of the city (11:22–24). Without the protection afforded by divine presence, the city is doomed to destruction.

The total execution of Yahweh's judgment is inescapable. There is no forgiveness, because the people have sinned individually and communally. The prophet declares that every segment of society has disregarded the obligations of the covenant. Ezekiel is comprehensive, including princes, priests, governmental officials, prophets, and the people of the land (the rural aristocracy) in a lengthy announcement of doom (Ezek. 22:23–31). Both male and female prophets are otherwise mentioned in an oracle in Ezekiel 13. The most serious accusations are made against King Zedekiah, who is declared the "wicked prince of Israel" who will receive "final punishment" (Ezek. 21:25–27; cf. chaps. 30–32).

In addition to singling out specified societal groups for destruction, Ezekiel addresses the community as a whole. The prophet recounts a history of sinful behavior—generational sin that occurred even during the exodus. In chapter 16 he depicts Jerusalem as a withering vine and as a foundling turned to prostitution. In chapter 23 he pictures the northern and southern kingdoms as siblings who turned to sexual promiscuity. The execution of Yahweh's wrath is comprehensive, in response to a series of sinful behaviors committed by every generation from the one that left Egypt up to the present one. Because of this, Yahweh declares famously, "[Son of Man], when a land sins against me by acting faithlessly, and I stretch out my hand against it, and break its staff of bread and send famine upon it, and cut off from it human beings and animals, even if Noah, Daniel, and Job, these three, were in it, they would save only their own lives by their righteousness, says the Lord GOD" (Ezek. 14:13–14).

The first half of the book focuses on destructive divine intentions. The uncleanliness of the people provides the impetus for Yahweh's behavior. Ezekiel's mission is to announce the coming disaster. Like a sentinel he simply declares the final verdict and warns of its advance, without offering any hope of avoiding it. Yahweh's wrath is coming to overtake the homeland. The sign-acts of Ezekiel visually portray the irreversible doom on Jerusalem and Judah. The idea that Yahweh stands in judgment over human sin is not a new one. What is significant and surprising is that Ezekiel singles out only part of the community for future judgment. He resoundingly condemns the people who remained in Judah and Jerusalem. Although much of the language in the first half of the book explicitly condemns the population in Judah, it has been argued that the passages about individual responsibility also indict the exiles in Babylon (14:12–20; 18:20–21) (Fishbane 1987). Ezekiel addresses the community in Babylon and carefully explains that their deportation and the destruction of Jerusalem stem from their own sin—not the sin of previous generations ("A child shall not suffer for the dignity of a parent" [Ezek. 18:20]) nor that of the Judahites in the land. However, punishment of the exiles has been accomplished by their deportation. Future judgment falls on Judah alone.

For Ezekiel, the judgment of Jerusalem is attributable to Yahweh alone and to no human army. His conception of Yahweh's intervention is informed by a heightened sense of the deity's majesty. Many of the phrases, "that you may know that I am the LORD" or "that I have spoken," conclude verses that depict the deity actively seeking to destroy the people in the land:

> My anger shall spend itself, and I will vent my fury on them and satisfy myself; and they shall know that I, the LORD, have spoken. . . . Moreover, I will make you a desolation and an object of mocking among the nations around you. . . . I, the LORD, have spoken—when I loose against you my deadly arrows of famine, arrows for destruction, which I will let loose to destroy you, and when I bring more and more famine upon you. . . . I will send famine and wild animals against you, and they will rob you of your children; pestilence and bloodshed shall pass through you; and I will bring the sword upon you. I, the LORD, have spoken. (Ezek. 5:13–17)

It is not surprising that in recent years concerns about the language of abuse in biblical literature have been raised (Darr 1992; Blumenthal 1993).

Ezekiel contends that in the final reckoning a holy deity can no longer be in contact with a people defiled by sin. There is no hope for the homeland. The primary image of Yahweh is as a divine warrior who brings about the downfall of the city. Like Lamentations, in which the poet depicted Yahweh both as an aggressor and as an abandoner, Ezekiel

shows how divine presence abandons the city of Jerusalem. However, unlike Lamentations Ezekiel relates the loss of the presence of Yahweh exclusively to cultic concerns. In chapter 11, the presence of Yahweh leaves the temple complex because it is defiled and the actions of the people have driven it away, not because Yahweh refuses to act on behalf of the people. Each disaster is directly attributable to the intention and action of Yahweh. With so great a respect for the deity and so little regard for the human being, how can Ezekiel hold out any hope?

Ezekiel's Hope

After receiving a report of the fall of Jerusalem, Ezekiel shifts his message to one of hope, especially in chapters 33–39:

> In the twelfth year of our exile, in the tenth month, on the fifth day of the month, someone who had escaped from Jerusalem came to me and said, "The city has fallen." Now the hand of the LORD had come upon me the evening before the fugitive came, but he had opened my mouth by the time the fugitive came to me in the morning; so my mouth was opened, and I was no longer unable to speak. (33:21–22)

This passage clearly overlaps with Ezekiel's call recounted in chapters 1–3 with the repetition of "the hand of the LORD had come upon me" and the theme of the prophet's speechlessness (Wilson 1972). Yahweh gives the prophet authority to speak a new word about future restoration. Hope for renewal includes return to the land, the reinstatement of the Davidic king, the restoration of the temple, and the reunification of Israel and Judah—ostensibly, the resumption of the political, social, and religious life of the nation. Only one sign-act performed by Ezekiel portrays a positive message. It deals with the reunited kingdoms under the aegis of a Davidic king, portrayed by the binding of two sticks (37:15–28). In addition, Ezekiel depicts Yahweh as the restorer of life. Examples of divine restoration include Yahweh as the good shepherd who protects the life of the sheep and brings them together once they have strayed (chap. 34) and the deity resurrecting dry bones (chap. 37). Ezekiel also portrays the return of the people in exile to the homeland (36:22–32). Once they are there, the land will produce the necessities of life in abundance as a sign of Yahweh's presence and protection. Hope lies in the character of a life-giving God who brings repatriation and renewal.

Two significant conceptions of restoration within Ezekiel's prophecy indicate future possibilities. The first emphasizes individual responsibi

for sin. Although discussed hitherto in conjunction with Ezekiel's message of judgment, this understanding of the fate of each person has a positive aspect. When persons are no longer judged for the sins of their forebears, sin and forgiveness become an individual concern (14:12–20; 18:20–21). Each person can have a relationship with Yahweh based on his or her response. This concept resonates with Jeremiah 31:29–30, but Ezekiel places a special emphasis on the individual before God. When speaking to Ezekiel, the deity calls into question the ideology of corporate responsibility by repeating a proverbial saying:

> The word of the LORD came to me: What do you mean by repeating this proverb concerning the land of Israel, "The parents have eaten sour grapes, and the children's teeth are set on edge"? As I live, says the Lord GOD, this proverb shall no more be used by you in Israel. (18:1–3)

Ezekiel's conception of individual responsibility is summarized by the assurance that each person alone bears responsibility for his or her wicked or just actions:

> Yet you say, "Why should not the son suffer for the iniquity of the father?" When the son has done what is lawful and right, and has been careful to observe all my statutes, he shall surely live. The person who sins shall die. A child shall not suffer for the iniquity of a parent, nor a parent suffer for the iniquity of a child; the righteousness of the righteous shall be his own, and the wickedness of the wicked shall be his own. (18:19–20)

The idea that no Judahite man or woman would be condemned for the sins of their ancestors contradicts the cyclical history of rebellion found in the Deuteronomistic History. It essentially frees each person from the burden of generational sin. On the one hand, it means that the present generation that experiences the destruction of Jerusalem is indicted in its collapse. On the other hand, the concept suggests that an individual has the ability to achieve a relationship with the deity based on his or her own behavior.

Associated with the idea of individual responsibility is a second concept important in Ezekiel: inner spiritual renewal. Ezekiel perceives that the onus for maintaining loyalty to the deity rests ultimately with Yahweh, who will provide the people with a new heart and a new spirit. A summary of this concept occurs in 36:26–27: "A new heart I will give you, and a new spirit I will put within you; and I will remove from your

body the heart of stone and give you a heart of flesh. I will put my spirit within you, and make you follow my statutes and be careful to observe my ordinances" (cf. 11:19; 18:31; and cf. Jer. 31). Although each person can respond to the presence of the deity, the emphasis is on the agency of Yahweh, who creates the opportunity for and enables the existence of relationality.

The prophet Ezekiel concentrated on explaining the fall of the nation and pointing to a positive future beyond disaster. Ezekiel's place among the Classical Prophets has been controversial, however, because his prophecies were mediated through a form more literary than oracular, his accusations against the people's unorthodox worship practices could reflect a time before Josiah's reform (usually associated with Manasseh's reign) rather than with the dates ascribed to the book, and the physical location of Ezekiel has often been disputed (was he in Judah or Babylon?). From the overview, it has become clear that Ezekiel fits well with that of his contemporary Jeremiah and along the lines of his prophetic predecessors. That said, there is one feature that sets Ezekiel apart from other prophetic literature. The book closes with an elaborate vision of the new temple, including a series of regulations regarding the building, personnel, and even the twelve tribes. Jeremiah may hold out hope for a reconstructed temple as Clements has suggested, but of all of the Classical Prophets, only Ezekiel creates a future vision that has clear regulations for its enactment. In this respect he is in line with the future vision of Deutero-Isaiah. Thus Ezekiel 40–48 will be the focus of the next chapter, where future visions take into account world events suggestive of a governance shift and as a result become more grounded in human response.

JEREMIAH AND EZEKIEL COMPARED

In some respects the prophecies of Jeremiah and Ezekiel are very similar. Both speak of judgment and salvation. Both perform sign-acts as one means of conveying their message. In addition, they envision the return of deportees to the land of Judah as a new exodus, describe a new covenant, condemn idol worship, rebuke immoral behavior and social injustice, and predict the return of the Davidic king. In line with the Classical Prophets of the First Temple period—Amos and Hosea, for example—Jeremiah and Ezekiel understand the destruction of Jerusalem and Judah as the fulfillment of the predictions of the Day of the Lord. According to Amos and Hosea, the Day of the Lord would entail the complete execution of divine wrath on a recalcitrant people. For Jeremiah, the day is one of calamity: "Like the wind from the east, I will scatter them before the enemy. I will show them my back, not my face, in the day of their calamity" (Jer. 18:17). In Ezekiel 7, the prophet declares:

> Your doom has come to you,
>> O inhabitant of the land.
> The time has come, the day is near—
>> of tumult, not of reveling on the mountains.
> Soon now I will pour out my wrath upon you;
>> I will spend my anger against you.
> I will judge you according to your ways,
>> and punish you for all your abominations.
> My eye will not spare; I will have no pity.
>> I will punish you according to your ways,
>> while your abominations are among you.
> Then you shall know that it is I the LORD who strike.
> See, the day! See, it comes!
>> Your doom has gone out.
>
> *(Ezek. 7:7–10)*

In other respects, the prophetic messages of Jeremiah and Ezekiel are different. Jeremiah is the suffering prophet, while Ezekiel is the dispassionate sentinel. In addition, the call narratives of the two men differ in the types of prophecy each is authorized to impart. Yahweh commissions Jeremiah to convey negative and positive words, including plucking up and tearing down, building and planting—in sharp contrast to Ezekiel's message, defined by lamentation, mourning, and woe. Although both Jeremiah and Ezekiel, according to the biographical information about them, stem from priestly families, Ezekiel is much more concerned about issues of orthodox worship and the purification of the cult. In addition, the ideology of the two prophets of the templeless age differs remarkably at points. According to Jeremiah, divine love and compassion—indeed forgiveness (Jer. 31:34)—provide the basis for the deity's will to redeem the people of ancient Israel. In contrast, in Ezekelian ideology the deity restores the people to the land and dwells in their midst solely out of regard for the divine reputation. The expression "so that you/they will know that I am the LORD" occurs close to eighty times in Ezekiel. Strikingly, Ezekiel never speaks of the deity's love or care.

Several factors together contribute to the sense that Ezekiel's message foretelling divine judgment is bleaker that that of the other prophets: the commission to proclaim judgment whether or not the people hear;

Ezekiel's location in Babylon, where he announces judgment on Judah, but speaks to his fellow exiles; and Ezekiel's heightened sense of the holiness of God, which distances the deity from the people. Unlike the Deuteronomic view, that entry into the land and the encounter with the Canaanites led to the incorporation of non-Yahwistic religious rituals, the view of Ezekiel is that the corruption of sin was present even during the flight from Egypt. Because of his bleaker portrait of divine judgment on Judah and his pessimistic view of the human person, recent studies have turned to consider the more negative outlook of Ezekiel's prophecy (see Schwartz 2000).

Another significant difference between the two books is in the conception of the presence of the deity (see Clements 1965; Mettinger 1982). Jeremiah, like the Deuteronomistic History, portrays Yahweh in heaven, but made available on earth via the name of the deity. In contrast, Ezekiel's thoughts on the presence of Yahweh is informed by the *kabod* theology of the first temple and the tradition of theophany. *Kabod* in Hebrew literally means "glory." Yahweh's glory is spoken of in three important sections of the book—in Ezekiel's call narrative (chaps. 1–3), in the vision of the defiled temple (chaps. 8–11), and in the vision of the restored temple (chaps. 40–48). These framing passages present the divine presence, literally the "glory of Yahweh," as mobile. In the call narrative, the glory of Yahweh travels to Ezekiel in Babylon to signify the presence of ancient Israel's deity outside the land (Ezek. 1:28; 3:12, 23). In the vision of the defiled temple, the *kabod* rises up from the temple and moves slowly and incrementally to hover on the outskirts of Jerusalem at the Mount of Olives—apparently repulsed by the unorthodox ritual practices taking place at the sacred site (Ezek. 10:18–19; 11:22–26). The movement of the presence of the deity symbolically seals the sanctuary's fate, because without divine protection and providence both it and the city are doomed. In the vision of the restored and purified temple that closes the book, the *kabod* of Yahweh returns to settle in the sanctuary (Ezek. 43:4–5; 44:4), and the city of Jerusalem is renamed "The LORD is There" (Ezek. 48:35). One of the more recent illuminating studies of the presence of Yahweh in Ezekiel is that of Kutsko, who reveals positive and negative aspects of divine presence, as well as the contrast between the active presence of Yahweh and the inefficacy of idols (2000). The presence of Yahweh in Ezekiel is made present on earth through the divine glory and not through a manifestation of the deity as in Deuteronomic name theology as understood by his contemporary Jeremiah.

The prophets Jeremiah and Ezekiel, who both lived through the harrowing events surrounding the fall of Jerusalem, provided messages that were timely as well as authoritative. From the prophet Jeremiah it is possible to understand how the divine word can have efficacy over time and in different circumstances. The fact that the words of Jeremiah could be used at different points in history and by another audience provides a positive indication of how divine possibilities are understood to be experienced through changing circumstances. Yahweh's word stands not in the remote past, but responds creatively to new situations. The prophet Ezekiel develops a slightly different message that is equally significant in its context. The *kabod* of Yahweh in his prophecies had destructive and constructive force: the loss of divine presence signaled the destruction of Jerusalem, while its return marked a new era of restoration. Ultimately for Ezekiel, a holy God requires a people committed to abiding by covenant stipulations.

CHAPTER 5

The Turn to Hope: I

Prophetic Visions of Divine Reversal

Up to this point, we have focused on literature that seeks the presence of God in the midst of Israel (the Psalms and Lamentations), records its history (Deuteronomistic History), and explains what appeared to be divine actions of punishment and the belief in future possibilities from and out of the complete and utter collapse of society (Jeremiah and Ezekiel). Toward the end of the templeless age—when dreams of returning to the homeland are more realistic or have even come about—the message shifts toward recognizing Yahweh's restorative purposes and speaking of the response of the vanquished community.

Scholars tend to associate the shift in focus at the close of the period with either the release from prison around 562 BCE of King Jehoiachin, who had been deported to Babylon during the first Babylonian incursion, or the appearance of King Cyrus of Persia in 550 BCE as a likely successor to the Neo-Babylonians. With either event, in the second half of the templeless age we find literature with a clear message of hope. A future outlook is expressed both in the positive, even jubilant message of Deutero-Isaiah and in Ezekiel 40–48, which perceives a new action by Yahweh and turns to regulating behavior to encourage covenantal renewal.

What is revolutionary about the literary record at this time is that the biblical writers take as their point of departure the reality that Yahweh is acting salvifically in their midst. They concentrate on how ancient Israel is to respond to Yahweh's faithful activity. Deutero-Isaiah sets the foundation for this belief with his prophecies that concentrate on hope. With a similar outlook, Ezekiel 40–48 turns to providing guidance to show

how people can live faithfully in relationship with the divine sovereign. The final chapters of Ezekiel have been considered to be an alternative vision of restoration to that propounded by Deutero-Isaiah. Together, the two visions of restoration provide the concerns that subsequent literature like that of Haggai, Zechariah, and the Holiness Code take as a starting point.

DEUTERO-ISAIAH (ISAIAH 40–55)

Scholars conventionally refer to Isaiah 40–55 as Deutero-Isaiah or Second Isaiah, because it represents a series of oracles by an anonymous prophet for whom the judgment of Jerusalem is in the past. His message speaks little of condemnation and turns instead to thoughts of future restoration and redemption. Deutero-Isaiah promotes belief in a change in circumstance: a tragic past is but a memory, and a bright future becomes discernible.

Although the book of Isaiah actually continues to chapter 66, due to a heading attributing the material to "Isaiah the son of Amoz" (Isa. 1:1), the entire book has been understood traditionally to be the work of one man—Isaiah of Jerusalem, who prophesied to kings Ahaz and Hezekiah in the eighth century BCE. It was already recognized, however, in the eighteenth and nineteenth centuries in Jewish and Christian scholarship that Isaiah 1–39 should be separate from chapters 40–66. The division between the two has been traced back to the medieval rabbinical commentator Ibn Ezra, who created a division based on thematic and historical grounds. The final chapters of the book deal with different issues and reflect a different time than chapters 1–39, which seek to enable Judah to steer clear of political entanglements. In 1892 the German scholar Bernard Duhm presented the main reasons to understand Isaiah 56–66 as a collection from a different hand and time than chapters 40–55. After that division, there remain three main units of the Isaiah tradition: chapters 1–39, associated with Isaiah of Jerusalem (Proto-Isaiah or First Isaiah); chapters 40–55, written by an anonymous prophet or prophets referred to as Deutero- or Second Isaiah; and chapters 56–66, a third collection written by an unknown Trito- or Third Isaiah around the time of the reconstruction of the temple. In addition, a vision of the end time in chapters 24–27 (called the Isaiah Apocalypse) is thought to be even later. The book of Isaiah in its final form contains a literary record spanning four centuries (from the eighth to fourth century BCE, as a conservative estimate).

The separation of Deutero-Isaiah rests partly on the large number of allusions in chapters 40–55 to chapters 1–39, but with slight differences in meaning. Two helpful analyses of this include those by Ronald Clements, who has studied the theme of blindness and deafness (1982a), and Hugh Williamson, who has studied the use of the term "the former things" by Deutero-Isaiah to refer to prophecies of judgment for Judah and Jerusalem recorded in First Isaiah (1994). References to and the reapplication of words, phrases, and themes used in chapters 1–39 with a variation in meaning suggestive of different circumstances provide some evidence in favor of the view that the prophecies of Isaiah of Jerusalem were carried on by a disciple or a school of disciples to speak to a new situation. Although it is profitable to analyze the prophetic messages of the three major collections of material in Isaiah individually (as will be done in this chapter in order to emphasize the thematic contribution to the period), beginning in the 1980s and continuing into the present there has been greater awareness of the contribution of each section to a unity of purpose. Indeed, the book appears to be the product of a concluding redactor who added passages to the beginning chapters of Isaiah (especially material located within Isaiah 1–6, e.g., 1:29–31) that shared common themes and vocabulary with the concluding chapter (especially, Isa. 66:18–24) as a way of enclosing the prophecies. Because of this unifying approach, it is certainly possible to study the book of Isaiah as a whole—perhaps even understood as a type of rolling corpus with prophetic authority, as Clements has argued. It is helpful therefore to keep in mind, when dealing with Deutero-Isaiah as a unit separated from the rest of the book, that it functions authoritatively as part of a whole series of Isaianic oracles that date from the eighth century onward.

The prophecies of Deutero-Isaiah arose during a time when suggestive world events were unfolding. The release of Jehoiachin and the successes of Cyrus contributed to a sense of expectation. The majority of scholars locate the prophet among the exiles in Babylon. A Babylonian provenance is suggested by prophecies of a return to the homeland. In fact, Deutero-Isaiah portrays repatriation as a return through the wilderness, like a second exodus, but on a grander scale than the former one from Egypt. In addition, the only oracle against the nation that appears in the prophetic collection condemns Babylon (chap. 47). In a close analysis of the historiographical literature of the period, Oded Lipschits has shown that hatred of Babylon like that found in Deutero-Isaiah is consistent with an exilic response (2005: 356–57).

In recent years a small but growing number of scholars have challenged the location of Deutero-Isaiah among the exiles. Confused geographical positions have raised questions about a setting in Babylon. For example, the exiles are depicted as coming from all the points of the compass rather than from Babylon (43:5–6; 49:12). In addition, the coming of Cyrus and the Persians as liberators of Babylon is spoken of as coming from the "north . . . from the rising of the sun" (41:25; cf. 41:2) and "from a far country" (46:11). These directions are rather odd if the writer was among the *golah*, as Persia is located to the southeast of Babylon. In addition to confused indications of place, themes within the collection are not thought to be consistent with a Babylonian setting. The complaint about Jacob/Israel's failure to offer sacrifice, for instance, has little bearing for the exiles, because foreign lands were thought to be unclean and unsuitable places for sacrificial activity anyway (43:22–24). Moreover, the depiction of Israel as "robbed and plundered . . . trapped in holes" does not call to mind a situation of deportation (42:22), and the focus on Zion/Jerusalem in chapters 49–55, on Judah (40:9; 44:26), and on rebuilding the temple (44:28) suggests the perspective of the homeland. The most outspoken proponent of the location of Deutero-Isaiah in Judah is Hans Barstad, who has produced a couple of monographs on this issue (1989; 1997). In addition to the points just raised, he argues that the new overland exodus motif functions in Isaiah 40–55 as a metaphor and is not meant to be physically accomplished. Furthermore, he argues that Judah is the location for the oracles based on recent evidence of community existence in the homeland.

There are certain problems with locating all of Isaiah 40–55 in Judah, however. None of the evidence advanced for a Judahite setting is completely uncontroversial. In terms of the confused geographical references, the writer may be speaking from the point of view of Judah without actually prophesying there. Ezekiel dates his oracles according to the years of King Jehoiachin, even though Jehoiachin no longer reigned during the time of Ezekiel's composition, and he visualizes Judah while not physically there. What is clear in the collection is that oracles in chapters 40–48 differ dramatically in tone, presentation, and ideology than those found in chapters 49–55. It has been suggested that the shift in emphasis reflects two settings: Babylon in the former and Judah in the latter. This suggestion benefits from recognizing the fit of the historical concerns of chapters 40–48 (the choice of Cyrus, oracle against Babylon, and the polemics against the idols) with a Babylonian setting. The latter chapters belong arguably in Judah. Note that the phenomenon of the alternation of the

Suffering Servant with Jerusalem personified as a woman (chapters 49–55) occurs elsewhere only in Lamentations, where Lady Jerusalem (Lam. 1 and 2) and a suffering strong man (Lam. 3) appear alongside each other. Interpreters have not noted this, however, as the figure in Lamentations 3 is not called a suffering servant, but a strong man. Nevertheless, the language used of the figure shares a significant amount of overlap with the third and fourth Servant Songs, as John Sawyer (1989) and Patricia Willey (1995, 1997) have shown. Because Lamentations is almost universally agreed to have been written in Judah, and Deutero-Isaiah shifts to convey prophecies more applicable to a setting in the homeland, it is possible that chapters 49–55 were written there as well.

In terms of composition, Deutero-Isaiah represents a prophetic message in a complex and undetermined structure. There is a wide range of views about how it achieved its present shape. A good survey is available in Joseph Blenkinsopp's commentary (2002). Another helpful introduction to the discussion is that of Rainer Albertz, who negotiates the many different theories of composition brought forward especially in German scholarship, in which delineations of the material are made on the basis of editorial activity (2003: 376–433). After a careful analysis of the viewpoints, Albertz suggests that there are two discernible conclusions in the material, at chapters 52 and 55. The concluding sections provide some evidence that there were two editions of the material, each with a distinctive message. Albertz refers to the first edition as DtIE1 (Deutero-Isaiah editor 1) and shows that it concentrates on proclaiming a joyful message of return to the exiles and comfort to Jerusalem. The second edition, termed DtIE2 (Deutero-Isaiah editor 2), emphasizes the power and endurance of Yahweh's word. The redaction-critical concerns enable a better understanding of the composition of the work, with Albertz taking seriously the very detailed work done by his colleagues in Europe.

Organizing the material according to overall themes, rather than attributing different authors, has been another approach favored in recent years. From this point of view it is possible to divide Isaiah 40–55 into two main sections based on themes not necessarily the result of two different hands. The first nine chapters (40–48) appear to be stylistically and thematically different from the last seven chapters (49–55):

40:1–48:22   Focus on historical concerns and including oracles to Jacob/Israel, diatribes and polemics against Babylon and idols, and hymns to Jerusalem and Cyrus

49:1–6   A hinge passage, classified as a Servant Song, representing the recomissioning of the prophet for a new task

49:7–55:13   Turn to ahistorical concerns and highlighting paradigmatic figures through oracles of salvation to Jerusalem/Zion, hymnic poems about the Suffering Servant, and hymns of restoration

Chapters 40–48 are referred to frequently as the Jacob or Israel section because of the frequency of the appearance of the terms "Jacob" and "Israel." Jacob/Israel represents a label for the people and is found fifteen times. These chapters have a more historical focus that sets them apart from the oracles found in chapters 49–55. In them, one prominent message focuses on the impending fall of Babylon: "Come down and sit in the dust, virgin daughter Babylon! Sit on the ground without a throne, daughter Chaldea!" (47:1). Another important prediction refers to the deliverance of the people. In Isaiah 40–48, the people are referred to as the "servant" twelve times (Isa. 41:8, 9; 42:19; 43:10; 44:1, 2, 21; 45:4; 48:20 et al.). In them, Yahweh recalls the special relationship with Jacob or Israel and instills a sense of hope in future possibilities: "But now hear, O Jacob my servant, Israel whom I have chosen!" (Isa. 44:1). Another distinctive feature of these chapters is the appearance of passages containing polemical statements against idolatry (40:19–20; 41:6–7; 42:17; 44:9–20; 45:16–17, 20; 46:1–7; 48:5). The prophecies about idols downgrade the divine status of deities other than Yahweh by depicting them as mere fashioned objects with no ability to effect change. A final development in chapters 40–48 that is not found in chapters 49–55 is the naming of the Persian ruler Cyrus as the earthly redeemer of Yahweh's people: "[the LORD says of Cyrus, 'He is my shepherd and he shall carry out all my purpose'" (Isa. 44:28; cf. 45:1, where Cyrus is termed Yahweh's anointed). The representation of the positive role of Cyrus within the deity's plans of restoration is startling, because foreign rulers in prophecies heretofore were featured in a negative way as the agents of Yahweh's destruction. Here, for the first time, a foreign ruler is even termed Yahweh's anointed. Yahweh appoints Cyrus to free the subject people, and he may be the figure called in 42:1–4 to enact the deity's righteous governance.

A second section of material is found in chapters 49–55. This section tends to be referred to as the Jerusalem or Zion section because of the attention paid to the city in these chapters. Prominent themes in chapters 40–48, such as the choice of Cyrus, polemics against idols, the historical situation of the exiles, the fall of Babylon, and the contrast between the former and the new things, make no appearance in the latter part of Deutero-Isaiah. Moreover, the figure of Jacob appears only in 49:1–6, which functions as a hinge between the two sections. Chapters 49–55 depict the continued unfolding of the hopes for restoration announced in chapters 40–48. The prophet, therefore, pays increased attention to ahistorical concerns, especially those having to do with the inner life of the community. Among the themes in these chapters are the gathering of Yahweh's people, the future of Israel, and the exaltation of Zion as the center of the deity's new kingdom. In addition, salvation oracles to and about Jerusalem, frequently portrayed as a woman in mourning (49:14–50:3; 51:9–52:12; 54:1–17), alternate with poems about suffering figures (49:1–13; 50:4–11; 52:13–53:12). The paradigmatic figures reveal Yahweh's continued concern and the value of suffering. The prophet visualizes the accomplishment of restoration as an overland exodus in which Yahweh forges a path through the desert to lead the exiled community home.

The Jacob/Israel (chaps. 40–48) and Jerusalem/Servant (chaps. 49–55) sections are held together by 49:1–6, where Yahweh commissions the prophet a second time (Williamson 1998). Because of the statement "I have labored in vain, I have spent my strength for nothing and vanity" (49:4), it is thought that the prophet was unsuccessful in his previous mission. From chapter 49 on, Yahweh appoints him as a light to the Gentile nations. Through the redemption of Jacob/Israel, the deity reveals divine omnipotence to the whole earth. Yahweh's sovereignty over the whole earth will be made clear through the prophetic mission:

> [The LORD] says,
> "It is too light a thing that you should be my servant
>   to raise up the tribes of Jacob
>   and to restore the survivors of Israel;
> I will give you as a light to the nations,
>   that my salvation may reach to the end of the earth."
>   *(Isa. 49:6)*

When discussing the literary composition of Isaiah 40–55, an important issue concerns the material classified as the Servant Songs, isolated by Duhm in his commentary on Isaiah. Four hymnic poems speak of a figure whom Yahweh designates for a particular role. The term "servant" appears in three poems (42:1–4; 49:1–6; 52:13–53:12), while one

(50:4–9) has the servant terminology added in a later verse (50:10). Duhm viewed these passages as songs about unspecified individuals that circulated as a group, independently from Deutero-Isaiah. The role applied to the figure contrasted sharply with references to "a/the servant" elsewhere, where triumphant language is used:

> Go out from Babylon, flee from Chaldea,
>> declare this with a shout of joy, proclaim it,
> send it forth to the end of the earth;
>> say, "The Lord has redeemed his servant Jacob!"
>>> *(Isa. 48:20)*

In the second through the fourth songs the servant is a figure who is increasingly downcast and anything but jubilant. In addition, the person in the servant passages tends to be cast as an idealized figure that contrasts sharply with the more generalized use of the servant elsewhere, who is portrayed as faithless and in need of encouragement (e.g., 42:18–25).

Some scholars concluded from Duhm's analysis that the songs were not an integral part of the message of Deutero-Isaiah and therefore contributed little to the thought of the prophet. Subsequent analysis has shown, however, that the Servant Songs are well integrated into their context (Mettinger 1983). Recent scholarship has concentrated, therefore, on how they contribute to the overall message of Deutero-Isaiah. How these poems function in Isaiah 40–55 rests to some extent on the identity of the figure. In the first so-called Servant Song, the deity addresses an unspecified individual whose mission is to the nations:

> Here is my servant, whom I uphold,
>> my chosen one, in whom my soul delights;
> I have put my spirit upon him;
>> he will bring forth justice to the nations.
>>> *(Isa. 42:1)*

Suggestions for the identity of the addressee include Cyrus, the prophet, and the nation or community of Israel. In the second poem, the Servant addresses the nations and relates a (second) commissioning:

> Listen to me, O coastlands,
>> pay attention, you peoples from far away!
> The Lord called me before I was born,
>> while I was in my mother's womb he named me.
>>> *(Isa. 49:1)*

The possible identities include the prophet and Israel. The Servant's soliloquy (the identification of the Servant as the speaker occurs in 50:10–11) in the third Servant Song recounts how the prophet or the nation has been rejected and abused for delivering its message:

> The Lord God Elohim has given me
>> the tongue of a teacher,
> that I may know how to sustain
>> the weary with a word. . . .
> I gave my back to those who struck me,
>> and my cheeks to those who pulled out the beard;
> I did not hide my face
>> from insult and spitting.
>
> *(Isa. 50:4)*

In the final Servant passage, the deity speaks of an individual whose suffering has redemptive value, even as the suffering of the nation has:

> Out of his anguish he shall see light;
> he shall find satisfaction through his knowledge.
>> The righteous one, my servant, shall make many righteous,
>> and he shall bear their iniquities.
>
> *(Isa. 53:11)*

The one who suffers even to death in the final two songs has been identified with the prophet and the people.

Although the Servant Songs vary to some extent, there is a design to their placement in the material that conveys something of the overall message of Deutero-Isaiah. Moreover, they borrow language from the royal court to appoint an individual (or group) to perform the work of Yahweh in the world. Through them, the prophet exemplifies Yahweh's continued care and provision. Appearing in the chapters that focus on the dawning of Yahweh's salvation, the first hymn records the designation of the deity's agent to bring about divine purposes. The second acts as a hinge in which the deity extends the commissioning of the prophet to include Yahweh's purposes for the whole world (in chaps. 49–55). The final two passages appear in a section that speaks words of redemption to mourning Lady Jerusalem. They reveal the redemptive nature of suffering as a means of explaining that the experience of the community after the collapse of Jerusalem serves a restorative purpose.

In our survey of the provenance and composition of Deutero-Isaiah, we have considered some examples of the message of the prophet, but it remains to be seen if this varied assortment of material conveys a coherent message. Peter Ackroyd divided the material into two types, noting on the one hand a focus on the acknowledgment of the execution of divine justice, and on the other hand a turn toward future restoration (1994: 118–37). The language of the book can certainly be viewed this way, as long as it is clear that for Deutero-Isaiah Yahweh's judgment is a thing of the past, and hope rests on divine intervention. In some respects, though, Ackroyd's division corresponds to categories that fit better with Jeremiah and Ezekiel, because in the main the anonymous prophet of Isaiah 40–55 proclaimed a jubilant message of hope for a despairing people. The various literary forms employed convey a consistent prophecy: first, that Yahweh is about to intervene miraculously, and second, that the deity can be trusted to redeem a suffering people (Kapelrud 1982; Albertz 2003).

Instead of a clear progression of thought, Deutero-Isaiah interweaves important ideas in an overarching message. The opening words of the collection disclose themes that will recur:

> Comfort, O comfort my people,
>   says your God.
> Speak tenderly to Jerusalem,
>   and cry to her
> that she has served her term,
>   that her penalty is paid,
> that she has received from the LORD's hand
>   double for all her sins.
> A voice cries out:
> "In the wilderness prepare the way of the LORD,
>   make straight in the desert a highway for our God.
> Every valley shall be lifted up,
>   and every mountain and hill be made low;
> the uneven ground shall become level,
>   and the rough places a plain.
> Then the glory of the LORD shall be revealed,
>   and all people shall see it together,
>   for the mouth of the LORD has spoken."
> A voice says, "Cry out!"
>   And I said, "What shall I cry?"
> All people are grass,
>   their constancy is like the flower of the field.

The grass withers, the flower fades,
   when the breath of the Lord blows upon it;
   surely the people are grass.
The grass withers, the flower fades;
   but the word of our God will stand forever.

(Isa. 40:1–8)

Because the verbs "comfort," "speak," and "cry" are in the plural, it is thought that the prophet has a vision in which he has overheard Yahweh speaking to the divine council in the heavenly court. Such a vision would be consistent with the call narratives of other prophets, such as Isaiah (chap. 6) and Ezekiel (chaps. 1–3), who envisioned the intersection of the heavenly and the earthly realms when they were commissioned. Deutero-Isaiah's observation of the discussion in the heavenly court reveals that punishment is a thing of the past, Yahweh is about to enter human history, divine intervention reveals Yahweh's sovereignty to the whole earth, the divine word accomplishes world-shaking and world-changing events, and the deity appoints him to prophesy. The prophecies concentrate on moving past the condemnation of Jerusalem toward the recognition that Yahweh is about to do a new thing by intervening in the world with plans of restoration. In addition, the call highlights the constancy of Yahweh's word by drawing a contrast with the transitoriness of human life.

The final verses in Deutero-Isaiah (55:6–16) repeat the theme of the reliability of the deity:

For as the rain and the snow come down from heaven . . .
so shall my word be that goes out from my mouth;
   it shall not return to me empty,
but it shall accomplish that which I purpose,
   and succeed in the thing for which I sent it.

(Isa. 55:10–11)

The call narrative and the closing words of Deutero-Isaiah emphasize the power and authority of the divine speech act relayed by the prophet (see 50:4–11). Not only is the word of Yahweh true; it accomplishes surprising changes in history.

The foundation premise of Deutero-Isaiah is that Yahweh is on the verge of entering human history to restore his people. Walter Brueggemann, in his study of Isaiah 40–55, analyzes the themes of exile and homecoming (1992: 90–108). In his view, it is organized around homecoming, but this theme actually underlines the prophet's message, as it is the premise of the collection. As such, thoughts of return and restoration appear throughout:

> I will bring your offspring from the east,
>> and from the west I will gather you;
> I will say to the north, "Give them up,"
>> and to the south, "Do not withhold;
> bring my sons from far away
>> and my daughters from the end of the earth—
> everyone . . . whom I formed and made."
>> *(Isa. 43:5–7)*

> For your sake I will send to Babylon
>> and break down all the bars.
>> *(Isa. 43:14; see vv. 15–21)*

> Go out from Babylon, flee from Chaldea,
>> declare this with a shout of joy . . .
> say, "The LORD has redeemed his servant Jacob."
>> *(Isa. 48:20)*

> Even to your old age I am he,
>> even when you turn gray I will carry you.
> I have made, and I will bear;
>> I will carry and will save.
>> *(Isa. 46:4)*

The motif of the return, pictured like a new exodus, supports the centrality of homecoming in Deutero-Isaiah.

In addition, the prophet speaks words of comfort to Jerusalem. He speaks of the rebuilding of the city and the refounding of the temple: "[The LORD] says of Jerusalem, 'It shall be inhabited,' and of the cities of Judah, 'They shall be rebuilt, and I will raise up their ruins' . . . and who says of Jerusalem, 'It shall be rebuilt,' and of the temple, 'Your foundation shall be laid'" (Isa. 44:26b, 28b). In other prophecies, the deity speaks words of comfort directly to Lady Jerusalem. She is told to shout about the return of Yahweh marching to the city with the exiles carried like lambs in the deity's arms (40:6–11):

> Get you up to a high mountain,
>> O Zion, herald of good tidings;

lift up your voice with strength,
  O Jerusalem, herald of good tidings,
  lift it up, do not fear;
say to the cities of Judah,
  "Here is your God!"
See, the Lord GOD comes with might.

(Isa. 40:9–10a)

The verbs are imperatives speaking to a female in 40:9, but commentators sometimes consider the herald to speak to Jerusalem. Because salvation oracles to the city personified as a woman appear in chapters 49–55 and Jerusalem (as the capital) was the chief city of Judah, it is unnecessary to understand the text differently than it is written. Elsewhere, the prophet responds to Lady Jerusalem's lamentations with words of comfort. To Zion's concern that "the LORD has forsaken me, my Lord has forgotten me," the deity draws on the depth of a mother's love and replies:

Can a woman forget her nursing child,
  or show no compassion for the child of her womb?
Even these may forget,
  yet I will not forget you.

(Isa. 49:14–15)

Lady Jerusalem—who when surveying the damage wrought by the Babylonians wept unconsolably with no one to comfort her in the book of Lamentations—finds her children restored:

The children born in the time of your bereavement
  will yet say in your hearing:
"The place is too crowded for me."

(Isa. 49:20–21)

Sing, O barren one. . . .
For the children of the desolate woman will be more
  than the children of her that is married, says the LORD

(Isa. 54:1, cf. 51:9–52:12; 54:2–17)

The words of the deity mediated through the prophet proclaim joyful tidings to the city bereft of its inhabitants and abandoned by its God (portrayed by the metaphor of divorce in 50:1).

While proclaiming the new thing that Yahweh is doing to restore a suffering people, the prophet silences any detractors by emphasizing reasons to believe in divine promises. Various features work together to convince an audience of the truth of the announcements of the prophet. In the first place, Deutero-Isaiah shows that Yahweh is the Creator deity who fashioned the cosmos as well as the earth. Depictions of Yahweh as all-powerful provide evidence in support of the prophet's claim that Yahweh can and will save. One means of encouraging belief in Yahweh's omnipotence is through what are classified as disputation passages. The disputation typically addresses the question of Yahweh's nature and ability to do what the prophet claims that the deity is about to do. In one, Yahweh is likened to a great giant who can hold all the world in the palm of his hand:

> Who has measured the waters in the hollow of his hand
>   and marked off the heavens with a span,
> enclosed the dust of the earth in a measure,
>   and weighed the mountains in scales
>   and the hills in a balance.
>
> *(Isa. 40:12)*

This use of rhetorical questions to make a point about the power of Yahweh to save appears throughout chapter 40 (vv. 13–17, 18–26, 27–31).

The prophet reinforces the conception of Yahweh as creator by contrasting Yahweh's creative ability to that of lifeless idols. Up until the collapse of Jerusalem, Yahweh was considered the supreme among many gods (monolatry rather than monotheism). In contrast to Ezekiel, who subtly denies gods divine status through literary strategies (see Kutsko 2000), Deutero-Isaiah is more forthcoming. In a variety of passages, he shows how the deities of other peoples are simply idols or statues that have no independent existence and cannot act. Yahweh alone is God. Polemical statements against the use of cultic images are characteristic of chapters 40–48. Idols are made by human hands (40:19–20; 42:17), unable to move about without being carried (46:1–7) and unable to predict or enable the execution of events (48:5), and those who consider carved and cast images as gods are stupid (42:17; 45:16, 20). In a long narrative passage, the prophet derides the creation of idols and the hands that fashioned them (44:9–20). In the description, he portrays the carpenter cutting wood for the deity's creation and using half of it to make a fire to roast meat and warm himself (44:18). Surely an object fashioned of wood cannot itself make.

Furthermore, the incomparability of Yahweh is made clear in the trial speeches against the nations. The trial speeches represent a genre that stemmed from the setting of the courtroom or the council of elders where a legal case is presented (41:1–5, 21–29; 42:18–25; 43:22–28). They too show the inefficacy of idols:

> Set forth your case, says the LORD;
>> bring your proofs, says the King of Jacob.
> Let them bring them, and tell us
>> what is to happen.
> Tell us the former things, what they are,
>> so that we may consider them,
> and that we may know their outcome;
>> or declare to us the things to come.
> Tell us what is to come hereafter,
>> that we may know that you are gods;
> do good, or do harm,
>> that we may be afraid and terrified.
> You, indeed, are nothing
>> and your work is nothing at all;
>> whoever chooses you is an abomination.
>> *(Isa. 41:21–24)*

In this trial speech, the supremacy of Yahweh is shown by the inability of other deities to respond to a challenge by ancient Israel's god. The pronounced monotheism in the trial speeches contributes to the prophet's argument about the credibility of Yahweh's word and ancient Israel's hope for the future.

Appropriately, evidence bolsters belief in the deity's power and intention to save. In the liturgy of the period, the sovereignty and might of the deity was never called into question. Instead, the community wondered if Yahweh would enter into relationship with them again. A second and possibly more forceful message in Deutero-Isaiah, then, turns to showing reasons why Yahweh is predisposed to save ancient Israel.

In the first place, Yahweh as creator deity established a relationship with a certain people. It is believed that through the events of the downfall of the nation, traditions about Yahweh's activities were linked together to provide a new understanding of the deity and divine interaction with humanity (we have seen examples of this trend in the Psalms). Deutero-Isaiah welded together the traditions of creation and election, concepts thought to have circulated independently before the kingdom's collapse (von Rad 1966). The prophet draws on creation myths of Yahweh's battle with the sea monster (sometimes referred to as *chaoskampf,* from the German "chaos battle") to establish authority. Alongside the depiction of the *chaoskampf* motif appear election traditions, including Yahweh's choice of a people (through the exodus), a king, and a capital city (Zion). The combination of the divine formation of the cosmos and the choice of a people occurs, for example, when the prophet speaks of the battle with Rahab and the crossing of the Reed Sea in one breath:

> Awake, awake, put on strength,
> O arm of the Lord!
> Awake, as in days of old,
> the generations of long ago!
> Was it not you who cut Rahab in pieces,
> who pierced the dragon?
> Was it not you who dried up the sea,
> the waters of the great deep;
> who made the depths of the sea a way
> for the redeemed to cross over?
> *(Isa. 51:9–10; cf. 44:24; 43:15–21)*

The prophet joins creation and election through the use of the title "Creator of the world" in conjunction with "Creator of Israel" (chap. 43; 44:2, 21; cf. 44:24; 54:5).

The language of kingship is also found democratized in the various oracles of salvation. These tend to begin with or include the expression "Do not be afraid" (41:8–13, 14–16; 43:1–7; 44:2–5; 54:1–8). The oracles of salvation were originally understood to stem from the rituals at the first temple, where the priest would offer a blessing on a worshiper in distress. An alternative explanation has been offered by Edgar Conrad (1985). He argues that the oracles of salvation are more accurately understood as stemming from the social setting of war. As such, they function as war oracles declaring victory, like those used to address Kings Ahab and Hezekiah in Proto-Isaiah (7:4–9; 37:6). In Deutero-Isaiah, the community becomes the recipient of the war oracles. For Conrad, the community is king.

To provide assurance of the deity's commitment the prophet draws on another tradition, associated with Zion as the place Yahweh chooses. The emphasis on Zion is shown by a concentration on oracles to the city predicting its renewal: Zion is destined to be rebuilt (44:26; 45:13; 49:14–15), to be the future home of Yahweh's scattered people (49:22; 45:14), and the city to which the nations make a pilgrimage in the eschaton (45:14–15; 49:22–23; 52:1–2).

The community can trust Yahweh's purposes for their future because of the intimate relationship between the two. Deutero-Isaiah coins an expression for the deity that foregrounds divine salvific intentions. The term "redeemer" occurs seventeen times throughout the collection (e.g., 41:14; 43:14; 44:6, 24; 54:5, 8), although it is completely absent in Isaiah 1–39. The word in Hebrew for redeemer (*goel*) stems from family law and stands for a family member who frees a relative from slavery/indentured service or rescues property lost through debt. A good example is found in the book of Ruth, where Boaz acts as the "kinsman redeemer" of Ruth. Applied to Yahweh, it appropriates familial language to insist that the deity is predisposed to rescue Israel from foreign enslavement. True to biblical tradition, Yahweh the redeemer appoints a human agent to act on his behalf:

> Thus says the LORD to his anointed, to Cyrus,
>   whose right hand I have grasped
> to subdue nations before him
>   and strip kings of their robes,
> to open doors before him—
>   and the gates shall not be closed:
> I will go before you
>   and level the mountains,
> I will break in pieces the doors of bronze
>   and cut through the bars of iron,
> I will give you the treasures of darkness
>   and riches hidden in secret places,
> so that you may know that it is I, the LORD,
>   the God of Israel, who call you by your name.
> For the sake of my servant Jacob,
>   and Israel my chosen.
>
> *(Isa. 45:1–4a)*

The prophet characterizes Yahweh as the redeemer par excellence in conjunction with the choice of Cyrus to enable the exiles to perceive that the deity's salvific plans are beginning to take place.

In attributing reasons for assuring the power and purposes of Yahweh to save the exiles in Babylon, Deutero-Isaiah drew on, created, and mixed various traditions. It is particularly in the conjoining of the creation and election traditions, but also with reference to other Zion traditions alone, that Deutero-Isaiah makes a powerful statement about Yahweh. In distinction to the cult of Marduk in Babylonia, where the deity's kingship was renewed annually in a ritual celebrating his victory over chaos waters, the prophet portrayed Yahweh acting in a salvific way through the course of time. In Deutero-Isaiah, creation at primordial time becomes the first action of Yahweh in history, but not the only one. Through a history of interaction with a particular people, Yahweh reveals his kingship over Israel. Indeed, Yahweh's work as creator paved the way for the election of Israel, the choice of the Davidic king, and Zion. In the current prophetic collection, the concept of Yahweh's lordship extends to include the whole world.

A powerful message to the people emerges whereby election traditions traditionally (and fomerly) applied to the Davidic king are redirected so that the community assumes the role of mediating Yahweh's presence to the world. The words of the Davidic covenant are democratized (Isa. 55:3–4) through the plural form of the imperatives (v. 3) and by the divine declaration "I will make with you (pl.) an everlasting covenant, my steadfast, sure love for David." The prophet extends to the community the eternal covenant of salvation and provision offered to the king. During the monarchic period, the Davidic king mediated the deity's presence to the people. After the new exodus, the people are to assume the role of king, as representatives of the deity in the world. They mediate to the nations the knowledge of Yahweh's presence.

Nevertheless, it should be born in mind that Deutero-Isaiah's thoughts on the place of the nations in the deity's purposes for humanity were not monolithic. Although the prophet raised the possibility that all the ends of the earth could turn to Yahweh to be saved (45:22) and extended divine salvation to the ends of the earth (49:6), more nationalistic sentiments occur as well. Consistent with this view are depictions of the nations as subservient to Israel (45:24–25; 49:22) and en route to Jerusalem in chains and bowing low (45:14; 49:17), even paying homage to the city by licking the dust of her feet (49:23). The light that the community sheds is such that the foreign nations will recognize the supremacy of Yahweh, but not be included in divine promises. The literature of the Second Temple period will continue to work out universal and national conceptions about foreigners (compare the inclusive messages of Jonah and Ruth with the exclusive agendas of Ezra and Nehemiah).

Concluding Thoughts on Deutero-Isaiah

Through his timely prophecies, Deutero-Isaiah provided convincing arguments of divine intervention. In so doing, he wove together the features of a hopeful vision that would serve as the impetus to return to the homeland. His words also functioned as theodicy. The final two Servant Songs portrayed the redemptive value of suffering to show that the execution of divine wrath provided a means to restore a troubled humanity to its deity. Moreover, the prophet elevated the people of ancient Israel to the status of the Davidic monarch in order to demonstrate that their exile had not been in vain. Rather than be regarded as humiliation, exile and repatriation would serve a constructive purpose by which ancient Israel would be a light to the nations, revealing Yahweh's sovereignty over the entire earth (42:6; 49:6; cf. 51:4).

Deutero-Isaiah draws attention to Yahweh's intentions by moving beyond disaster, explaining ruination as judgment for sin fully paid for, and highlighting plans for restoration. He also reassures the community that Yahweh intends to act on its behalf. In a powerful vision of future salvation, the collection grounds conceptions of the deity in mythology and salvation history. The message of Deutero-Isaiah hinges on an awareness of the new and wondrous act Yahweh is about to perform in the world on captive Israel's behalf. He foresaw and faithfully prophesied divine reversal. His future vision failed, however, to include concrete descriptions of how an event of the magnitude described would come to pass or what it would entail for the future. That would be the task of other visionaries of the time.

EZEKIEL 40–48

There is widespread agreement that the final chapters of Ezekiel should be regarded as a separate set of prophecies, in spite of close affinity with chapters 1–39. For the purposes of examining the visions of restoration that would set the stage for the final years of the templeless age, Ezekiel's vision of the restored temple and community in chapters 40–48 will be considered in conjunction with the message of Deutero-Isaiah.

The final chapters of Ezekiel contain a vision of restoration that centers on the temple at the heart of the community. With its concerns about the reconstruction of the sanctuary and regulations regarding its use, chapters 40–48 lie close in thought and language to the Priestly material of the Pentateuch. As such, they may date from a time slightly later than the prophecies of Ezekiel or even represent the writing of a different hand. Against the separation of the final chapters from the rest of the book, Greenberg has stressed that as a priest Ezekiel would be expected to show concern for temple restoration and, in fact, had prophesied its renewal in earlier material (Ezek. 20:40; 37:24–28). In addition, the concluding chapters complement the vision of the heavenly temple that began the book in chapter 1 and the vision of the earthly temple corrupted and in need of destruction found in chapters 8–11. Although these chapters can profitably be included within a discussion of Ezekiel, they are slightly different in tone and concerns. They provide an idealized portrait of a time beyond disaster that complements the picture of Isaiah 40–55. Deutero-Isaiah provided the reasons to perceive a cosmological shift in which Yahweh was on the verge of intervening in a decisive way on behalf of exiled Israel. In conjunction with Deutero-Isaiah's emphasis on divine reversal, Ezekiel provides a practical message relating how the community should reorganize itself with a focus on Yahweh and how it must carefully regulate worship in order to honor the deity.

The material about the restored temple has three main sections:

40:1–43:12   Vision of the future temple
44:1–46:24   Regulations governing access to the temple and
　　　　　　　　cultic activity
47:13–48:35 The apportionment of the land among the people

As was the case with Ezekiel's vision of the earthly temple, he is transported by a divine hand to a very high mountain overlooking the city of Jerusalem. In the vision, a heavenly being guides him around the newly constructed site from the east gate. The vision includes its measurements, the return of the divine glory of Yahweh to dwell in its midst, and the resumption of burnt offerings. In addition, it provides lists of regulations for entry into the sanctuary and for the apparel and behavior of the officiating priests. Life-giving waters flow from the rebuilt temple, which provides the centerpoint of the restored community.

Belief in Jerusalem as the place of the presence of Yahweh is linked in Ezekiel 40–48 with priestly concerns about the sacred and the profane. The two are intertwined out of necessity. The glory (*kabod*) of Yahweh could return to the temple and settle within ancient Israel (43:1–12) only if the sanctuary was protected from all impurity. The final chapters of Ezekiel, therefore, concentrate on regulations for temple construction and its cultic personnel. Interestingly, the description of the rebuilt sanctuary demonstrates that its architectural design secures purity (40:1-43:12). For instance, it is divided into three spaces by walls and steps to demarcate increasing degrees of holiness. Entrance to the different levels of holiness is made possible through a series of doors that control access to the inner and outer courts. The doors are magnificent in proportion, surpassing the dimensions of the fortified gates of cities excavated in recent years. The overall impression conveyed by them alone is that of a fortress. Access to the Holy of Holies in the innermost part of the temple is strictly controlled in order to safeguard its sanctity and thus the presence of Yahweh.

Other measures are in place to protect the holiness of the sanctuary. There are strict regulations governing cultic personnel, and a hierarchy of function is imposed. Further, the sanctuary is depicted in many respects like the Solomonic temple, but on a much grander scale. Its dimensions are larger and its elevation higher. Unlike the previous temple, it does not lie adjacent to the king's palace, but in a separate portion of holy land, away from the royal residence. In monarchical times it comprised a single complex with the royal palace. The placement of the restored temple safeguards it from contamination by the king. Interestingly, the separation of the sanctuary from the royal residence correllates to how the prophet understood kingship in restored Jerusalem. Ezekiel did not deny completely the powers of the monarch; instead, he curtailed them, especially when compared to the situation in the First Temple period, when the king participated in and led worship services. Even the terminology changes to signify diminished responsibility: Rather than denoting the ruler a *melek*, "king," Ezekiel 40–48 speaks of him only as a *nasi*, "chieftain or leader." The term *nasi* is found most prolifically in premonarchical texts, where it signifies a tribal leader (see the classic study by Speiser 1963). The political authority of the king decreases in Ezekiel's vision of the new period of divine governance. Similarly, the king is no longer the mediator of the cult as in the First Temple period. His access within the temple precincts is limited, and he is included among the laity (Ezek. 46:10).

Through an analysis of chapters 40–48, Jon Levenson has argued that the restored temple vision bears a remarkable degree of overlap with the Priestly version of the Sinai event, in which Moses saw a vision of divine presence and received detailed instructions for the construction of the tabernacle (Exod. 24–31) (1976). Even as Moses emphasized the concept of a holy nation to a group of liberated slaves, so Ezekiel specified the availability of Yahweh's presence in the future to those who were on the verge of return from Babylon. Ezekiel's experience presented a programmatic vision of correct behavior for the exiles upon their return to Jerusalem. The deity's sanctuary will be at the center, physically and spiritually. The twelve tribes are redistributed in concentric circles around the temple. Furthermore, it is the only body of laws in the Hebrew Scriptures not placed in the mouth of Moses. The location of legal material in the final chapters of Ezekiel ratifies the prophet's words and acts as a programmatic vision for the future. The regulations demonstrate to the community restored to Jerusalem how it can renew its covenantal relations with Yahweh.

CONCLUSIONS

The visions of restoration in Deutero-Isaiah and Ezekiel 40–48 take as their departure the recognition of Yahweh's imminent intervention and are complementary. Deutero-Isaiah concentrated on delivering a twofold message: first, to stir the community to return home, and second, to comfort a despairing people. The prophet's message remained in some respects unrealistic, in that it provided no concrete details about how the people were to travel home and what they should do once there. Deutero-Isaiah's portrait of an exodus march led by Yahweh through the wilderness with valleys raised up and mountains made low surely inspired, but it provided little practical detail. In contrast, Ezekiel recognized that a future in the homeland was impossible without clear instruction. He concentrated on how the community should organize itself in order to honor Yahweh and dwell in the deity's favor. The right ordering of society, with the temple at its center, was imperative, as was individual behavior that took seriously the holiness of Yahweh.

The prophetic messages of Deutero-Isaiah and Ezekiel 40–48 mark a significant shift in the literature of the templeless age. Yahweh is about to perform a new act in history. In response to the imminence of divine intervention, Deutero-Isaiah bolsters belief while Ezekiel 40–48 focuses on ways in which the community could act as and remain the people of Yahweh. Both, however, remained utopian.

In the next chapter we will see how Deutero-Isaiah's vision of divine reversal and Ezekiel's concerns with religious and social regulation are taken up in the literature from the time of temple renewal.

CHAPTER 6

The Turn to Hope: II

Commitment to Covenant

The fervor that suffused the prophetic literature of Deutero-Isaiah and Ezekiel 40–48 was given fresh expression in the writings of Haggai and Zechariah 1–8 and in the Holiness Code (H) of the Priestly work. These documents speak of a new action by Yahweh and turn to regulating behavior in an effort to encourage covenantal renewal.

What is revolutionary about the literary record at this time is that the biblical writers take as their point of departure the reality that Yahweh is acting salvifically in their midst. They concentrate on how ancient Israel is to respond to Yahweh's faithful activity. Deutero-Isaiah and Ezekiel 40–48 set the foundation for this belief with prophecies that concentrate on homecoming and restoration. Their prophecies provide the two points of departure that literature at the close of the period will share. The prophetic writings of Haggai and Zechariah 1–8 take as their departure point the belief that Yahweh's purposes are breaking into history and the need for Israel to respond in the light of divine commitment. The Holiness Code turns to providing guidance to show how people can live faithfully in relationship with the divine sovereign, Yahweh.

PROPHETIC ENCOURAGEMENT

Haggai

Haggai is one of the twelve so-called Minor Prophets—a collection of prophetic books edited together in what is called the Book of the Twelve (Nogalski 1993). Until the twelve shorter prophetic books were unified (sometime in the Persian period), the prophecies of Haggai were joined to Zechariah (chaps. 1–8) by a chronological framework. Haggai, whose name means "my festival," prophesied during a four-month period in 520 BCE. Because of concerns about agricultural matters and exhortations aimed at the people in general, it has been suggested that he had remained in Judah following the downfall of the state (Beuken 1967; Bedford 2001). Unlike his counterpart Zechariah, Haggai represented the perspective of the Judahites that remained in the land following the downfall of Jerusalem.

Although the book of Haggai is only two chapters long, it has undergone a series of critical inquiries whose results remain important in any introduction to the book. It has long been recognized that the oracles of the prophet are surrounded by an editorial framework (Ackroyd 1951, 1952; Mason 1977; Beuken 1967; Tollington 1993). Passages in which the prophet directly speaks to the people and/or their leaders appear in 1:2, 4–11, 13b; 2:3, 6–9, 11–14, 15–19, 21–23. An editorial framework has been delineated at 1:1, 3, 12, 13a, 14, 15; 2:1, 2, 4–5, 10, 20, with 2:2, 4–5 remaining disputed. The additions share features and terminology in common with Chronicles, Ezra, and Nehemiah. It has been suggested that the Chronicler (that is, the author of the books of Chronicles and possibly Ezra and Nehemiah) edited the book of Haggai. In his monograph, Willem Beuken argued instead that Haggai and Zechariah 1–8 had been edited in a Chronistic milieu (1967). In a close analysis of the language of the Levitical sermons found in Chronicles, Rex Mason has provided an alternative way to view the relationship between the prophets and the history (1990). He concludes that the editorial framework of Haggai and Zechariah shares language and themes with what he suggests are more appropriately called the addresses in Chronicles, rather than sermons. Furthermore, the editorial framework provides an indication that Haggai's prophecies were "preserved in circles which claimed him as one of the preachers playing a most important role at a critical stage of the people's history, a stage in every way parallel in significance to the times of Moses and David" (Mason 1990: 194). The prophecies of Haggai (and later Zechariah) were collected, edited, and transmitted by priests who elucidated sacred traditions to the community in the sanctuary as the preachers of the second temple.

Beyond giving an indication of the use of the prophecies of Haggai in the cult, the editorial framework provides a precise chronology for his appearance. He prophesied over a four-month period during the second year of the reign of King Darius (520 BCE). The dates conveniently divide the book into four sections: chapter 1; 2:1–9; 2:10–19; 2:20–23. In the first section, the prophet exhorts the community to rebuild the temple (1:1–15). He carefully explains that the people's failure to construct the sanctuary has led to divine displeasure and continued judgment in the forms of famine and poverty. The populace responds to Haggai as a true prophet and proceeds to build: "And the LORD stirred up . . . the spirit of all the remnant of the people; and they came and worked on the house of the LORD of hosts, their God" (Hag. 1:14).

Subsequently, the prophet focuses attention on divine restoration that accompanies the rebuilding (2:1–9). Yahweh shows favor by blessing the efforts with the divine presence: "Work, for I am with you, says the LORD of hosts, according to the promise I made you when you came out of Egypt. My spirit abides among you; do not fear" (Hag. 2:4–5). The deity's reassurance bolsters the builders and further adds a future promise to bring the treasure of the nations to beautify the temple (Hag. 2:6–9). In the third section, the prophet appeals to the priests to provide a ruling on purity and impurity as a means to symbolize that a cursed and defiled people will be blessed when the temple has been restored (2:10–19). Finally, Haggai announces divine plans to overturn the world order and reinstate a Davidic king on the throne of Judah (2:20–23). The prophecy to Zerubbabel is interesting in that it inverts the typical order of kingship and temple construction as found, for example, in the First Temple period and in other literature of the ancient Near East. Only after Yahweh has assumed the divine throne will a leader be appointed for Judah. Elsewhere, the king served as the temple builder who established a place for the deity to inhabit subsequently. In Haggai, the deity and the community are the temple builders.

Two main themes run through the book. The first has to do with the importance of the construction of the sanctuary. The second shows that following its foundation, Yahweh promises renewal and restoration. Haggai's oracles concerning the reign of Yahweh have been discussed in terms of an eschaton or a future vision at the end of time (Childs 1979; Ackroyd 1994), but are better understood as a natural consequence of the reestablishment of a place for the presence of the deity (Bedford 2001). As such, Haggai's predictions of divine presence and providence will materialize in historical time, rather than at an unspecified end time.

In sum, the prophecies of Haggai serve a practical function in fostering the recognition of Yahweh's turn toward restoration and encouraging temple construction. Although the prosperity promised to the sanctuary has been linked to material possessions (Clines 1994), like his prophetic predecessors Haggai understands the Jerusalem sanctuary to be the deity's residence and so imbued with divine presence and glory (Hag. 1:3). The correlation of the famine with the failure to rebuild the temple—that is, the correlation of judgment with disobedience—suggests that for Haggai the rebuilding of the sanctuary has more to do with the relationship between the deity and the people. As Bedford has suggested, Haggai alerts the people that the period for the execution of divine wrath is waning. Obedience to the deity's will results in the reestablishment of the covenant and the restoration of divine presence. So temple construction has more to do with embracing Yahweh's favor than with a simple connection between the deity and material wealth. A people favored by Yahweh will no longer experience the judgment of ruination. As Yahweh's presence provides for the community, so it will for the temple. Haggai's thoughts bear a striking resemblance to the Deuteronomic principle that disobedience to the prophet as the spokesperson of God leads to destruction and judgment, whereas obedience leads to Yahweh's goodwill meted out through divine provision.

Although David Winton Thomas in the Interpreter's Bible series asserted that "Haggai has no claim to be ranked with his great predecessors in the prophetic office" (Thomas 1956: 1039), he single-handedly inspired the rebuilding the temple. His prophecies alerted the community to the dawning of Yahweh's favor and the end of divine displeasure. The history of the Second Temple period owes him a great debt, in spite of the brevity of his activity.

Zechariah 1–8
Inextricably linked with the prophecies of Haggai are those of Zechariah, who likewise regarded the reconstruction of the temple as a vital element of a restored Jerusalem. It is generally agreed that only chapters 1–8 belong to the prophet active at the end of the sixth century BCE (known sometimes as Proto-Zechariah or First Zechariah), although chapters 9–14 (Deutero-Zechariah or Second Zechariah) evidence a continuity of thought (Childs 1979: 355–72; Mason 1976; Smith 1995: 124–25, 133–38). The prophetic activity of Zechariah overlaps that of Haggai, but continues longer, from 520 to 518. Zechariah is of priestly lineage (Zech. 1:1, cf. Ezra 5:1; 6:14) and is thought to have returned with Zerubbabel from exile in Babylon (Neh. 12:4, 16, via Zechariah's patronym, Iddo). His inclusion among the first few waves of repatriates explains one of the aspects of his prophecies that differs from Haggai. In contrast to his contemporary, who never spoke explicitly of the return of the exiles, Zechariah maintains a consistent focus on the divine call for their repatriation.

Chronological statements at 1:1, 7 and 7:1 divide the book of Proto-Zechariah into three units. A lengthy section of fantastic and other-worldly visions in 1:7–6:15 is surrounded by an introduction in 1:1–6 and messages relating the visions to the community in 7:1–8:23. The introduction rehearses the past unfaithfulness of Israel and serves as warning to the present generation that just as Yahweh punished their foreparents, the deity will judge their iniquity. Their hope rests on contrition and repentance. The introduction is followed by a series of eight visions that the prophet received in one night (1:7–6:15) that clarify the important role ascribed to the temple and the city of Jerusalem. Along with the establishment of the city come the cleansing of the priesthood, the return of the exiles from Babylon, and the rebuilding of the temple. The final two chapters (chaps. 7–8) combine the themes of judgment and restoration. In spite of the fact that the people have failed to keep the covenant with Yahweh in the past, which resulted in their being subject to divine judgment and scattered to the nations, the deity will return to Jerusalem. As a result of the return and the dwelling of the divine presence (*kabod*, "glory") in Jerusalem, there will be peace in the city, the exiles will return and be included among the covenant people, the temple will be rebuilt, the land will be made fruitful, the community will become righteous, and all nations will be blessed through the people of Yahweh.

Like Haggai, Zechariah 1–8 has been edited. In certain material the prophet is referred to in the third person (1:1, 7; 7:1, 8), in 1:1 and 7 the title "the prophet" is added after his name, and a chronological framework organizes the material. In addition, explanatory oracles attached to the night visions appear to act as a corrective to another interpretation: the cleansing of the high priest Joshua in 3:6–10, the address to Zerubbabel in 4:6b–10a, and the appendix to the entire series of visions in 6:9–15. Mason has shown that, like the additions in the book of Haggai, the added material (1:1–6; 3:6–10; 4:6b–10a; 6:9–15; 7:4–7, 8–10, 11–14; 8:1–8, 9–13, 14–17, 18–23) reflects a homiletical milieu slightly later than the time of the prophet (Mason 1990: 197–234.). Like the editorial framework in the book of Haggai, the passages lie close in thought to the addresses in Chronicles. They confront the challenge of understanding the failure of Haggai and Zechariah's promises regarding divine intervention to materialize by projecting the period of salvation into the future.

The night visions of Zechariah stem from the prophet and indicate divine purposes for Jerusalem and for the nations. The first vision provides an overview of the main themes that will be brought out in the others. Through the vision of the four horsemen patrolling the earth (1:8–13) and the accompanying explanatory oracles (1:14–17), the prophet reveals that the period of divine wrath has come to an end. Yahweh has come to Jerusalem with compassion and directs his anger towards the nations who acted too harshly in the overthrow of Judah. The second vision comments further on the nations, depicted as the four horns, and their judgment by the four smiths or Yahweh's agents (2:1–4 = ET 1:18–2:1). The third vision presents Yahweh's commitment to Jerusalem: to protect it with his abiding presence and to reside within it (2:5–9 = ET 2:1–5). An oracle in 2:10–17 (= ET 2:6–13) recapitulates the themes found in the first three visions: call to the exiles in Babylon to return, Yahweh's actions on ancient Israel's behalf to limit the might of the nations, and the divine return to Jerusalem, followed by the institution of universal dominion. Following the first series of visions, Zechariah sees the authority invested in the priestly ruler Joshua (3:1–10, generally agreed to be a later insertion) and the Davidide Zerubbabel (4:1–6a, 10b–14). Through the visions of the fly-ing scroll (5:1–4) and the woman in the basket (*ephah*) carried by female winged creatures to Babylon (5:5–11), the prophet clarifies proper com-munity activities in the new age of Yahweh's rule. While the scroll seeks out and eliminates those who fail to abide by societal regulations, the agents of Yahweh in the vision of the basket return the personification of idolatry to Mesopotamia. Although the exact referent of the woman in the basket is ambiguous, she is clearly a goddess.[1] The final vision in 6:1–8 parallels the first in its depiction of four colored horses (although here appearing with chariots). Through the reappearance of similar content and ideology, it creates an envelope structure that sets the visions apart. As in 1:8–13, the horsemen survey the earth as a sign of Yahweh's divine sovereignty.

David Petersen has provided a helpful analysis of how these strange scenes function as part of the prophet's message (Petersen 1984). In the first place, they suggest that the divine reversal of current abysmal affairs is happening already on a cosmic level. Zechariah is made aware of the divine plans and encourages the community to continue working on the temple in anticipation of them. Second, after comparing various points of contact between the visions and Ezekiel 40–48, he suggests that the night visions create a counter (perhaps, complementary) restoration program that shifts its focus to pragmatic societal concerns. The visions provide ways for the community to reorganize itself.

---

1. Interestingly, the rhetoric that depicts the elimination of the worship of a goddess in Judah corre-sponds to a phenomenon apparent from the material culture of the time. The production of the female fig-urines used for votive purposes, called the Judahite pillar figurines, ceased in the early part of the fifth century BCE.

Another helpful analysis of the night visions is that of Carol and Eric Meyers (1987), who focus attention on their organization. Based on the widely agreed belief that the fourth vision in chapter 3 was an insertion from a later time and the first three visions correspond thematically to the last three, Meyers and Meyers perceive a concentric structure that focuses attention on the fifth vision (the lampstand and the olive trees), which is located centrally, along with the inserted vision, which draws attention to the purification and installation of Joshua, the high priest. The organization of the scenes suggests that the temple and the leadership of the community were significant features in the (edited) prophetic message.

In addition, the way the visions function within the book as the means of conveying Zechariah's message raises an interesting point about the nature of prophecy at the close of the templeless age. Meyers and Meyers have asserted, "All told, the complex organization of the visions stands out as a unique contribution of Zechariah to the Hebraic tradition of the prophetic vision" (1987: lviii). Of the Classical Prophets, Amos, Jeremiah, and Ezekiel had visions; however, they were interspersed within other types of material more consistent with prophecy elsewhere. Zechariah's visions are more elaborate and are the sole vehicle of his message. The reasons for the shift are unclear, but it may have its basis in growing awareness of the transcendence of Yahweh (to distance the prophet from direct contact with the deity), in the associations made between divine revelation and temple rebuilding as found in ancient Israel[2] and elsewhere in the ancient Near East (see Meyers and Meyers 1987: lviii; Bedford 2001), or as a means of authenticating Zechariah as a true prophet of Yahweh.

Proto-Zechariah should be considered a precursor to apocalyptic literature because of the centrality of the visions and of the certan features, such as the appearance of an angelic messenger to interpret the visions and the abstract symbolism of the heavenly visions. On the latter, Zechariah differs from Isaiah (chap. 6) and Ezekiel (chaps. 1–3), who saw a representation of the deity on earth (in the temple in Isaiah and among the exiles in Babylon in Ezekiel) in that he sees symbolic scenes in the heavens as in apocalyptic literature. However, Zechariah remains at variance with apocalyptic thought, which placed divine rule and recompense at the end of history, projected far into the future. Instead, Zechariah 1–8 understood Yahweh's salvific commitment to ancient Israel to be on the verge of happening in the unspecified, near future.

---

2. In the Hebrew Bible, Yahweh revealed the plan of the tabernacle to Moses in Exod. 25:8–9, and Solomon dreamed of the sanctuary in Gibeon in 1 Kgs. 3:5–14.

Because Haggai had been successful in generating work on the temple, Zechariah focuses on encouraging the continuation of building. The prophecies of Zechariah contain an inverted message to those of Haggai. Whereas Haggai understood the period of divine presence and providence to begin following the construction of the temple, Zechariah understood that the inbreaking of Yahweh had begun, thus mandating the construction of the sanctuary. The basis of Zechariah's message is that the physical restoration of Jerusalem leads to a spiritual renewal of everything connected with Yahweh's presence. From Jerusalem Yahweh's glory will radiate to all the nations of the earth.

SUMMARY OF THE PROPHETIC CONTRIBUTION
TO THE THOUGHT OF THE PERIOD

In the prophets discussed in the previous chapter, we saw how the oracles of Deutero-Isaiah left open the way in which the return of the exiles and the restoration of Jerusalem would come about, while those of Ezekiel 40–48 painted an idealistic portrait of restoration concerned with the proper worship of Yahweh. On a clear continuum, Haggai and Zechariah proclaim the conclusion of the period of Yahweh's judgment and encourage the community to rebuild the temple in recognition of that fact. Haggai's argumentation differed from Zechariah's in that he understood the completion of the temple to be the necessary precursor to the inbreaking of Yahweh's dwelling presence and the blessings such an event would hold. In contrast, Zechariah understood the period to be dawning already and thus urged the community to continue its efforts in recognition.

A variety of studies have used the books of Haggai and Zechariah in a historical task to ascertain the character of the community that lived in the years that close the templeless age. Some scholars see a developing schism in the community based on differences between the repatriates and those who had remained in Judah (Hanson 1975; Meyers and Meyers 1987; Weinberg 1992; Lipschits 2005) and find possible imperial reasons for temple construction (Meyers and Meyers 1987; Weinberg 1992). Moreover, some recent studies of these prophets have led to a series of skeptical remarks about the whereabouts of Zerubbabel. The disappearance of the Davidide (a feature more pronounced in Proto-Zechariah) has suggested to some the possibility that he fell out of favor with the Persians and was removed from office. As Zerubbabel played an important part in the prophecies of Haggai and Zechariah, further questions have been raised about a desire to instigate open rebellion against Persia.

A recent consideration of these issues by Bedford, however, has found each theory wanting in certain respects (2001).

In refuting the various theories of controversy, Bedford has shown more fully the type of ideological interpretation upon which the prophets Haggai and Zechariah 1–8 drew. In the first place, he shows that the initiatives proposed by Haggai and Zechariah remain consistent with the overturning of the events that transpired during the collapse of the nation. Each seeks the return of Yahweh to Jerusalem (implied in Hag. 1:8; Zech. 1:16; 2:14, 16–17=ET 2:10, 12–13; 8:3); understands the renewal of Yahweh's presence to signify divine sovereignty over the earth accompanied by the shaking of the heavens, the earth, and the kingdoms (Hag. 2:6–7, 22; Zech. 2:13=ET 2:9); correlates the restoration of divine kingship with the return of the human king (Hag. 2:20–23; Zech. 3:9b; 6:13); and the return of Yahweh's rulership blesses the temple, land, and people (Hag. 2:6–9, 18–19; Zech. 8:4, 12–13), while Zechariah adds the repatriation of the exiles to Jerusalem (Zech. 2:10–14=ET 2:6–10; 8:7–8) (Bedford 2001: 232–33). In claiming the overturning of signs of divine displeasure, Haggai and Zechariah draw on traditions prevalent in monarchical Zion theology (Bedford 2001; see also Mason 1990). Both Haggai and Zechariah link temple rebuilding to the concept of the king-ship of Yahweh found, for example, in the Zion psalms (46, 48, 76), the enthronement psalms (47, 93, 96–99), and other psalms that reflect divine kingship (24, 29).

Although Haggai and Proto-Zechariah draw on monarchical temple and royal ideology, they stress different aspects of the tradition. In addi-tion to the Psalms, Haggai drew on the northwest Semitic myth of the storm god (normally associated with Ugarit's Baal), who establishes his rule by defeating the sea monster (Yam), as well as the prophetic tradi-tion of the oracles against the nations (cf. Amos 1–2; Isa. 13–23; Jer. 25:24–38; 46–51; Ezek. 25–32).[3] From Ezekiel, he draws out the theme of the judgment of the nations. In distinction, instead of appealing to the myth of the storm god's battle to establish supremacy or the judgment of the nations from the Psalms, Zechariah uses language consistent with an alternative prophetic tradition in which the nations gather to worship Yahweh in Jerusalem/Zion. Both prophets refract monarchical royal ide-ology through prophetic traditions in order to indicate that it is the cor-rect time to proceed with temple construction. One of the concerns of

---

3. The storm god's victory is marked by the building of his temple, where he sits enthroned on the moun-tain of his choosing. In Canaanite mythology, Baal's sacred mountain is Mount Saphon.

the literature of the period (as found in the lament psalms and the book of Lamentations) rested on how long the deity would persist with divine anger. Both Haggai and Zechariah answer the question by declaring the end of divine judgment and the dawning of Yahwistic favor.

Bedford's contribution to the understanding of the traditional nature of the rebuilding ideology of Haggai and Zechariah is important in many respects, but for our purposes it shows how the prophets at the close of the sixth century correspond well to the prophecies of Ezekiel 40–48 and Deutero-Isaiah, along with the traditions that circulated in the First Temple period. As such, their activity fits better with the templeless age than with the Second Temple period. They are the bridge to the period of the Second Temple in that both sought to encourage the community to refound the sanctuary in Jerusalem, but they share little with the determinative thought of Ezra and Nehemiah. Neither Haggai nor Zechariah referred to the community in such a way as to suggest they understood a division among the people. Both are inclusive in their terminology and their visions of the restored community. Even the fact that the two books were joined together suggests something about the character of the time, as Haggai represented the perspective of the land and Zechariah that of the exiles. The Judahites in the land and the repatriates joined together in a unity of purpose.

A measure of support for this view has been provided by Yair Hoffman's analysis of Zechariah's discussion of the fasts (2003). Zechariah describes four fasts that took place during Neo-Babylonian rule: "Thus says the LORD of hosts: The fast of the fourth month, and the fast of the fifth, and the fast of the seventh, and the fast of the tenth, shall be seasons of joy and gladness, and cheerful festivals for the house of Judah: therefore love truth and peace" (Zech. 8:19). According to tradition the fasts commemorate the siege of Jerusalem, the breaching of its walls, the destruction of the palace and the king, and the murder of Gedaliah. Because the exiles in Babylon would not have commemorated the death of Gedaliah, Hoffmann has argued that the fasts indicate that when deportees filtered home, efforts were made to align the worship practices of the repatriates and those who had remained in the land of Judah. He perceives the attempt to create a national identity against the backdrop of a divided society, but Haggai and Zechariah—when viewed without ideas imported from Ezra 1–6—show no evidence of a schism.

Deutero-Isaiah provided the impetus to conceive of a return to Jerusalem from exile in Babylon. He supported his declaration of restoration by highlighting the features of Yahweh's character that enabled trust and by explaining how the suffering of deportation and loss had redemptive value. However, his vision remained abstract. Haggai and Zechariah pick up where his message left off by indicating the dawning of Yahweh's favor and the necessary human response to divine salvation. In the period of salvation, Haggai and Zechariah urge the community to embrace the restorative purposes of Yahweh and live as a covenant people fit for the presence of the deity in their midst: Haggai urges the priority of the temple and Zechariah turns to societal relations. Theirs marks a new kind of hopeful vision that remains consistent with that of Ezekiel 40–48 in that they account for the fitness of the community to exist in relationship with Yahweh.

TORAH

The Holiness Code

General introductions to the exilic age include the Priestly Code (the material in Genesis to Numbers attributed to a source concerned with priestly matters) among the literature of the period. The Priestly Work (P) outlined the history of ancient Israel from the creation of the world in Genesis 1:1 to just before entry into the promised land. Since Julius Wellhausen originally defined P as one of the four sources of the Pentateuch in the nineteenth century, the discussion has moved in significant new directions. The intertwining of the narrative and legal material of P was associated traditionally with the Babylonian exiles because it exhibited priestly concerns with genealogies, dates, laws, and cultic regulations. P was thought to have provided an alternative history to prior sources (J and E) by placing law and religious ritual at the community's inception. The composition includes stories that function to establish the relationship between Yahweh and the people Israel, to participate in identity formation, and to provide legal material to enable Israel to remain without blemish in the presence of a holy deity. It is true that the thought underlying P probably has its origin in the experience of the collapse of Jerusalem and the loss of the land. Nevertheless, recent theories posit the conclusion of the work to well beyond the sixth century BCE. For instance, a growing number of interpreters focus on questions about the possible influence of Persian administrative policies on its formation.

Because the final formation of the Pentateuch likely stems from a time well after the templeless age, it will not be considered in this study. However, although P was conceived of as a history, the writers clearly drew on prior material to construct their story. In the center of the Torah is the book of Leviticus, which contains a series of what appears to have been independent older materials shaped into a comment on the experience of the downfall of Jerusalem, with particular concern for those who had experienced the martial tactic of exile. The Holiness Code represents a portion of the P material that is most often linked to the sixth century BCE. The Holiness Code, or H, is a recognizable block of material in Leviticus 17–26 that shares an unswerving focus on the holiness of Yahweh and requirements for correct social relations within ancient Israel. The term itself stems from August Klostermann, who in 1877 defined it as "a law of holiness" (*das Heiligkeitsgesetz*). Although the conception of H as a separate collection of legal material contained within the Priestly work has lost adherents in recent years (notably, Rendtorff 1986: 145; Gerstenberger 1996: 17–19), the majority of scholars continue to regard it as a recognizable law code. In his examination of the rhetoric directed at the people and the land in H, Joosten has indicated four arguments in favor of viewing it as a distinct corpus:

1. Like other law codes it begins with prescriptions concerning the place of sacrifice (Lev. 17).
2. It concludes with a series of blessings and curses (Lev. 26).[4]
3. Paraenetic elements occur throughout to explain the laws to a current generation.
4. Vocabulary, style, and theology distinguish chapters 17–26 as a separate entity (Joosten 1996: 6–7; see also Driver 1891: 43–55).

H also contains units of older material arranged and expounded by a final redactor to respond to the collapse of Jerusalem and thoughts of the resettlement of the land.

Although it seems possible to speak of the Holiness Code, scholars have encountered difficulties in identifying its date, provenance, and relationship to the Priestly material found in Genesis, Exodus, Leviticus (chaps. 1–16, 27), and Numbers. Since Martin Noth, it has been generally agreed that H included older legal materials formulated into a unit during the templeless age by the exiles in Babylonia. Suggestive of this period is its commonality with Ezekiel in the depiction of the otherness and holiness of Yahweh, as well as the similarity of the final three escalating curses in its closing chapter with the events that took place (including mass deportation) around the fall of Jerusalem. A major challenge to

---

4. Comparable legal collections elsewhere include the book of the covenant (Exod. 20:22–23:33), considered to be the oldest collection of laws in the OT; Deuteronomy (particularly chaps. 12–26); and Ezekiel 40–48.

the consensus view came out of the doctoral dissertation of Israel Knohl (1987; 1995), now expanded and defended by Jacob Milgrom (1991, 2000, 2001; cf. Ross 2002). Knohl argued that H belonged to the eighth century and acted as the influence for Hezekiah's reform (2 Kgs. 18)— much in the same way Deuteronomy (or a part thereof) functioned as propaganda for the Josianic reform a century later (2 Kgs. 22–23). In his analysis of the Priestly work, Knohl noted texts that shared points of contact with H, including Exodus 6:6–8; 31:13–17; Leviticus 11:44–47; and a portion of the book of Numbers. This material he attributed to a Holiness school that reworked the Priestly Torah and to which the final redaction of the Pentateuch belongs.

In spite of Milgrom's support, the precedence of P to H and the redaction of P by H have failed to shift the view of the majority of scholars. Two points that raise questions about it deserve mention here. Baruch Levine (2003) has shown that an original text about the presentation of display offerings in Leviticus 23 (vv. 9–11, 14, 15–17, 20–22) was modified to conform with the festival rites in P (by the additions of vv. 12–13, 18–20; cf. Lev. 1–7). In showing the addition of material consistent with Priestly traditions, such as the inclusion of burnt sacrifices and festal chronology, Levine has provided an important defense of Wellhausen's ascription of the composition of H before the completion of the Priestly work. Following an alternative line of argumentation, Graeme Auld (2003), likewise, has raised one problem with Knohl's view. In his examination of Exodus, Leviticus, and Numbers as distinct entities (with a view to assessing the message of each), he provides a clear rationale for the priority of H over P. He noted that the increased role of the Levites in Numbers, marked by their appearance throughout the book (chaps. 1, 2, 3, 4, 7, 16, 17, 18, 26, 31, 35) and the duties attributed to them, is at odds with their almost complete absence from Leviticus. In H, references to them occur only in Lev. 25:32–34, in conjunction with Levitical property. Attention to Levitical priests changes in the literary deposit. Around the time of Chronicles, Ezra, and Nehemiah, more attention is paid to their role in the cult. The increased number of references to the Levites in Numbers, as opposed to their rare mention in H, suggests H was written before the Priestly composition. Auld's insight positions Numbers (and P's continued editing) to a time later than H that, although belonging to literature consistent with Levitical thought, fails to contain much interest in the Levites themselves.

The consensus view of the priority of H to P can be upheld, but its provenance requires some additional thought. Knohl and Joosten regard it as a product of the First Temple period, but several arguments suggest that this is not the case. First, in addition to thematic similarities between Ezekiel and H, there are striking vocabulary parallels, as S. R. Driver has indicated (1891). Moreover, Walter Zimmerli has shown that there are reasons to link the "circles" that formed H with those that transmitted the book of Ezekiel in its final form (1979: 52). He discusses the two in terms of cross-communication and fertilization. Furthermore, because the final chapters of Ezekiel (40–48) exhibit a priestly hierarchy that never existed after the dedication of the temple in 515 BCE, the final date for the completion of Ezekiel must predate the refounding of the sanctuary in Jerusalem, when priests would have resumed their duties (Clements 1982). The correspondence of language and mutuality of ideas between Ezekiel and H positions them as contemporaries. In addition to what appears to be the exchange of ideas between Ezekiel and H, the exhortatory message of Leviticus 26 clearly speaks to the situation of exile. As Peter Ackroyd has recognized already, the chapter (esp. vv. 33–39) not only envisions an exilic situation, but presents an interpretation of it (1994: 85–86). Finally, the Holiness Code retains a future vision with respect to restoration that would suggest a date before the reconstruction of the temple. In only one statement is an explicit declaration of Yahweh's future plans for the community made, and that is with reference to the land (Lev. 26:42).[5]

Of its structure, Ackroyd stated, "The whole section is by no means unified" (1984: 88), because it includes a number of smaller units and independent collections of laws. The incorporation of laws dating from before the final compilation of the work may hinder the application of an organizing rubric. Nevertheless, in a recent analysis of the book of Leviticus, Christopher Smith has argued that narrative sections appearing in chapters 8–10 (the description of the ordination of priests), chapter 16 (the Day of Atonement), and 24:10–23 (the narrative of the blasphemer) divide the legal material into recognizable sections (Smith 1996). In his view, there are four sections of legal material (chaps. 1–7; 11–15; 17–24:9; 25–27) separated by three sections of narrative.

The benefit of the scheme Smith proposes is that it organizes the material into units of thought and corresponds to a noticeable technique employed in the rest of the Priestly work. One objection to his theory is

5. Kratz 2005: 109–14, argues that the Holiness Code forms part of early additions to the Priestly Work. In his view H stems from the time of the Second Temple and provides its theological program. His view is not completely incompatible with the inclusion of H among the literature of the templeless period. Even if the final form of H and its inclusion in P stem from a time later than the sixth century, it is clear that its composition was inspired by and, indeed, related to the fall of Jerusalem.

that he includes chapter 27 in H, which is generally agreed to end at chapter 26. It is clear that chapters 25 and 26 are linked. In contrast to the other chapters in Leviticus 17–27, chapter 26 alone fails to contain a heading, which indicates that it is a continuation of chapter 25. Moreover, chapter 25 begins with a unique heading. Elsewhere, according to the Hebrew text each chapter opens, "the LORD spoke to Moses, saying" (17:1; 18:1; 19:1; 20:1; 21:1;[6] 22:1; 23:1; 24:1; 27:1). Chapter 25 begins with a statement that mentions Mount Sinai "the LORD spoke to Moses on Mount Sinai, saying" (25:1). The mention of Mount Sinai in 25:1 forms an inclusio with the concluding statement of chapter 26: "These are the statutes and ordinances and laws that the LORD established between himself and the people of Israel on Mount Sinai through Moses" (26:46). These details show that chapters 25 and 26 are one literary unit.

Although Smith has argued that chapter 27 continues the theme of redemption from chapter 25, it is clear that the meaning of the concept differs. In chapter 27, redemption is contained in a section that concentrates on regulations for vows. Also, the concluding chapter includes the term "holy," but without the relational overtones found in chapters 17–26. The dual focus of chapter 27 on holiness and redemption, along with the formulae of vows, suggests that it serves as an appendix to the whole of Leviticus. As such, it draws together themes from H and from the Priestly writer. The majority view of scholars who understand chapter 27 as an epilogue can be upheld.

Smith's analysis of Leviticus is helpful, nonetheless, in that it highlights different emphases in the two parts of the material (17–24:9 and 25–26). In chapters 17–24:9, issues of holiness and impurity take pride of place. However, chapters 25–26 shift to the idea of redemption, stemming from the loaded Hebrew term *goel*, "kinsman redeemer," linking it with Yahweh's remembrance of the land and the covenant with Abraham, Isaac, and Jacob (26:42).

In the main the laws in H deal with regulations concerning cultic matters (issues of proper sacrifice, regulations concerning the priests, festivals, and various procedures) and social concerns (interpersonal relations of a sexual or business nature, as well as the fair treatment of resident aliens, foreigners, debt slaves, and other slaves).

Since the work of Albrecht Alt on legislation, it has been common practice to divide the laws into categories (1989). Apodictic law contains

---

6. Leviticus 21:1 contains a slightly expanded version of the heading. The Hebrew text reads, "Yahweh said to Moses: Speak to the priests, the sons of Aaron, and say to them: No one shall defile himself for a dead person among his relatives."

a divine imperative for behavior either as a direct command, "You shall not . . . ," or as a curse, "Cursed is the one who . . . " or "'Whoever does . . . will be put to death." The best examples of apodictic law are found in the Ten Commandments (Exod. 20:1–17; Deut. 5:6–21). Another type of law develops a model for behavior based on making an example from a situation and the penalty imposed in connection with it. Based on cases, this type of material is classified as casuistic law. It represents a type of civil law common to the nation-states of the ancient Near East. A third type of material—more along the lines of moral guidelines—reflects human-itarian interests of the type that have to do with the treatment of slaves or resident aliens (e.g., Exod. 22:21). Finally, the largest corpus of legal material in the Torah deals with matters relating to practices of a reli-gious nature; these can be classified as cultic laws.

Comparative studies of biblical law with that found elsewhere in the ancient Near East have shown that there is a certain commonality in type and concerns. The most famous parallels are the series of laws found on the stele of the Babylonian King Hammurabi, dating from the second millennium BCE. Through comparison with ancient Near Eastern legal material, another type of law can be added to the above categories, that of vassal treaty (see McCarthy 1978). A vassal treaty is made between two nations with one exerting power over the other. The more powerful entity promises to protect its treaty partner as long as it continues to abide by regulations made in the agreement, such as giving tribute in the form of foodstuffs or wine, refraining from alliances with other nations, and not rebelling against the overseeing nation. Vassal treaties outline the requirements of both parties, as well as a series of infractions that would require a punitive response by the powerful nation. The most famous example of this type of agreement in the Old Testament is the covenant between Yahweh and the people Israel, but treaties of this sort are mentioned elsewhere (e.g., 2 Kgs. 16–18). They reflect the nature of the relationship of the northern and southern kingdoms with the impe-rial powers of the Canaanite and Mesopotamian regions. H contains a series of laws that correspond to most of these types.

Within H the most important point of interest for our purposes has to do with holiness as a feature of 17:1–24:9. The underlying premise of H is that Yahweh is a holy deity (20:7, 26; 21:8) whose name is holy (20:3; 22:1, 31). Although features of the deity beyond the ascription of holiness remain undisclosed, for H, the fact is that Yahweh exists. The phrase "I am the LORD" recurs throughout the collection (18:5, 6, 21; 19:14, 16, 18, 28, 30, 32, 37; 20:8, 26; 21:8, 12, 15, 23; 22:2, 3, 8, 9, 16, 30, 31, 32, 33; 26:2, 45).

In H, however, the holiness of Yahweh is never an abstract concept distanced from historical reality. Each appearance of the holiness of Yahweh corresponds with legal regulations for the people of ancient Israel, phrased positively or negatively. Positively, the holiness of the deity makes it imperative that the people are holy: "You shall be holy, for I the LORD your God am holy" (19:2); "Consecrate yourselves therefore, and be holy; for I am the LORD your God" (20:7). On the other hand, behaviors that violate the covenant call Yahweh's holiness into disrepute. By disrespecting Yahweh, the people profane the deity's holy name: 'You shall not give any of your offspring to sacrifice them to Molech, and so profane the name of your God: I am the LORD' (18:21; cf. 20:2–3); "You shall not steal; you shall not deal falsely; and you shall not lie to one another. And you shall not swear falsely by my name, profaning the name of your God: I am the LORD" (19:11–12; similarly to the priests 21:6; 22:2).

In addition to the use of Yahweh's holiness to encourage the observance of rules of behavior, H emphasizes the relationality of Yahweh to the people. Of instances where Yahweh is mentioned, a startling number associate the deity and the community. In fact, "I am the LORD" qualified by "your God" occurs twenty-two times (18:2, 4, 30; 19:2, 3, 4, 10, 25, 31, 34, 36; 20:7, 24; 23:22, 43; 24:22; 25:17, 38, 55; 26:1, 13, 44). Commands and regulations are mentioned in conjunction with its appearance as well. There are positive statements, "My ordinances you shall observe . . . I am the LORD your God. You shall keep my statutes and my ordinances; by doing so one shall live: I am the LORD" (18:4–5), and negative imperatives, "So keep my charge not to commit any of these abominations that were done before you, and not to defile yourselves by them: I am the LORD your God" (18:30; cf. 18:21). A similar type of phrasing combines positive behaviors with negative ones to refrain from (19:3–4). Moreover, Israel is to act holy because their deity is a holy deity: "You shall be holy, for I, the LORD your God, am holy" (19:2). Even more important to H is the concept that the sanctity of the people stems not from their own worth, but from the deity's actions: "Keep my statutes, and observe them: I am the LORD: I sanctify you" (20:8; of the priests, 21:8; of the high priest in all but name, 21:15; of those with blemishes among the priests, 21:23). Sanctification has at its heart the concept of separation from the unclean; therefore, other terminology occurs in the collection where Yahweh separated the people to himself (20:24, 26).

All of the statements about the deity's holiness and the divine relationship with the people lead ultimately to the basis of the regulations in the Holiness Code. If one underlying premise in H is divine holiness, the second principle rests securely on the relationship between the deity and the people. For H, a special bond was forged in the events of the exodus: "I am the LORD, your God, who brought you out of the land of Egypt" (19:36; 25:38 cf. 25:42–46). The fullest expression of this concept combines sanctification, the identification of the former slaves of Egypt with Yahweh, and legal obligations:

> Thus, you shall keep my commandments and observe them: I am the LORD. You shall not profane my holy name, that I may be sanctified among the people of Israel: I am the LORD: I sanctify you, I who brought you out of the land of Egypt to be your God: I am the LORD. (Lev. 22:31–33)

The events of the exodus take place in order to transfer the allegiance of slaves in Egypt to Yahweh (25:38): "For to me the people of Israel are servants; they are my servants whom I brought out from the land of Egypt: I am the LORD your God" (25:55; cf. 25:42) (Joosten 1996). The regulation of communal and religious behavior establishes the conditions for the treaty (known more biblically as the covenant) between Yahweh and the people. Yahweh promises, "I will maintain my covenant with you" (26:9). The fullest expression of the inextricable link between the holiness of Yahweh, the choice of the people of Israel, and the exodus includes the rubric "And I will walk among you, and will be your God and you shall be my people. I am the LORD your God who brought you out of the land of Egypt, to be their slaves no more; I have broken the bonds of your yoke and made you walk erect" (26:12–13).

The inclusion of the liberating event in Egypt has at its conclusion the occupation and maintenance of the land. Chapters 25 and 26 both include the importance of the promised land as the signifier for the relationship with Yahweh. In chapter 25, the correlation of the observance of the law and existence in the promised land is made: "You shall fear your God; for I am the LORD your God. You shall observe my statutes . . . so that you may live on the land securely. The land will yield its fruit and you will . . . live on it securely" (25:17–19) and summarized: "I am the LORD your God, who brought you out of the land of Egypt, to give you the land of Canaan, to be your God" (25:38). In chapter 26, it becomes clear that irreverent behavior results in an escalating series of curses, culminating in the loss of the land and deportation: "Then the land shall enjoy its sabbath years as long as it lies desolate, while you are in the land of your enemies; then the land shall rest and enjoy its sabbath years" (26:34). Exile does not mark the final destiny of the people, because a new future is made available through confession (26:40–41). H closes with the possibility of a future based on the permanence and trustworthiness of the deity who entered into a covenant with the patriarchs (26:42) and Moses (26:45). Remarkably, the covenant in H is no new covenant, as in Jeremiah and Ezekiel and as implied in Deutero-Isaiah's motif of the new thing coming to pass. The covenant remained unbroken: "Yet for all that, when they are in the land of their enemies, I will not spurn them, or abhor them so as to destroy them utterly and break my covenant with them; for I am the LORD their God' (26:44).

The Holiness Code contains a remarkable message of the relationship between the deity and the covenant people and of his purposes for them. H rests on the sovereignty of Yahweh; hence the repeated insistence of "I am the LORD," to which can be added "and there is no other" or "who brought you out of the land of Egypt." Yahweh alone is God—the supreme deity over the cosmos and history, but intimately connected with a people, through thick and thin. The legal material that predominates serves as an indication of ways the people can live in a reverential relationship with their deity and continue to enjoy the privileges of that special relationship (especially as it entails life in the promised land of milk and honey). It helpfully sets out guidelines for religion and society that enable a fulfilling and ongoing relationship between Yahweh and a community separated for his worship.

In addition, H serves also as a defense of the deity. The expression "I am the LORD" appears in the divine revelation to Moses in the Priestly narrative (Exod. 6:2, 6, 7, 8) and in conjunction with Moses's first ascent to Mount Sinai (Exod. 31:13). The giving of the law written by the deity on two stone tablets appears in conjunction with the stipulation of Sabbath observance as the sign of the covenant between Yahweh and the people. The Sabbath is given as a symbol for the Israelites to remember that "I am the LORD who sanctifies you." Because of the identification of Yahweh as the deity who brought the slaves from Egypt and established a covenant with them at Mount Sinai, the agreement between Yahweh and the community is the precept underlying the Holiness Code in its entirety. A measure of support for this interpretation arises from the consideration of the placement of Leviticus (with H within it) between the story of the erection of the tabernacle in the wilderness at Mount Sinai (Exod. 34–40) and the departure from Mount Sinai (Numbers). The appearance of Leviticus between the establishment and disassembly of the tabernacle at Mount Sinai strongly suggests that its legal material should be regarded as a continuation of the laws given by Moses. For the writer of H, Yahweh never rejected the covenant. It underwrites the text and is, therefore, echoed in each of the fifty occurrences of "I am the LORD." The promises of the deity remain steadfast even when events in history call them into question.

The Holiness Code and Contemporary Literature

Several additional reflections on the Holiness Code show that it fits alongside the literature of this period, particularly that of the prophets of restoration. In general, the hortatory final chapter considers the critical juncture in the people's history to be the moment in exile when the choice to recognize communal failure and confess generational and individual sin came to the fore (26:40–41, 43). Heartfelt repentance provides the means for Yahweh to remember the covenant with Abraham, Isaac, and Jacob (26:42, though oddly written in reverse order) and the commitment made in the events of the exodus (26:45).

Moreover, H shares the outlook of Haggai and Zechariah 1–8 in certain respects. In the first place, the agricultural concerns of H parallel those of Haggai. Second, there does not appear to be a division in the community along the lines found at the time of Ezra and Nehemiah, who separated the people of the land and foreigners from inclusion in the community. As Joosten has shown in his comprehensive analysis of the language addressed to the people and the land, the community is defined by inclusion rather than exclusion. Israel for H is an ethnic entity, dependent on birth, among which resident aliens are welcome.[7] Finally, like Deutero-Isaiah, the Holiness Code exhibits a democratic perspective. Although the writer cites regulations for the priests, they are held in no higher esteem than the people.

Based on theological and linguistic affinities between the circles that produced H and those that produced Ezekiel, Clements has argued further that H "is a form of literary commentary and adaptation of Ezekiel's prophecies particularly directed towards the hope of restoring the Jerusalem cultus. It emerged among the Babylonian exiles, and very probably from within the circles of the exiled Zadokite priests of Jerusalem. . . . It extended and applied [Ezekiel's prophecies] to provide a mandate for the restoration of the Jerusalem temple cultus in anticipation of the time when it would once again become necessary" (Clements 1982: 132). The regulations of sacrifices and festivals (Lev. 22–25:9), the emphasis on the relation-

---

7. See Middlemas 2005 for a discussion of a community defined by cultic identity, but inclusive of foreigners, in Isa. 56–66.

ality of Yahweh, and the significance of worship[8] support Clements's suggestion. H is programmatic. One feature that suggests its purpose as a mandate for renewal is the repetition of the phrase "When you come into the land" (Lev. 19:23; 23:10; 25:2). Like Haggai and Zechariah, whose prophecies sought in the main to provoke and encourage the reconstruction of the temple in Jerusalem, the Holiness Code served a similar purpose among the exiles (whether in Babylon or upon their return).

SUMMARY OF THE LITERATURE AT THE CLOSE OF THE TEMPLELESS AGE

The jubilant Deutero-Isaiah provided a vision of restoration with particular attention to the return of the exiles characterized as a new exodus. His message countered the uncertainty expressed in Lamentations with words of comfort and assurance. Moreover, the salvation oracles spoke of divine intentions for repatriation and renewal. Both messages depended on conceptions of the deity that served to bolster its claims and reassure a populace languishing in exile. Beyond claiming the imminence of divine actions for the future, Deutero-Isaiah provided few pragmatic details. The allusions to the exodus and the specific claims of a new exodus provided a grand, if unrealistic, scheme. Its focus was on the journey rather than the homecoming.

Ezekiel 40–48 and Leviticus 17–26 each provided visions of the homeland that supplemented the idealism of Deutero-Isaiah. Jon Levenson has shown that Ezekiel 40–48 provides a programmatic vision for the reconstruction of society in Jerusalem that placed religious observance at the center of the restored community (1976). These chapters suggested further that the organization of the new community would have at its heart the proper worship of Yahweh. Such would enable the continued presence of the deity in the midst of the community and the protection and sustenance that would provide.

The Holiness Code likewise established a plan for the restored community that would emphasize the proper observance of social justice and religious rituals. It set out clearly how the people were to remain faithful partners in the covenant with Yahweh. As a complement to Ezekiel's restoration vision, its message of the relationality of Yahweh focused attention on Yahweh's commitment to the people.

---

8. A concern with worship is stated in "You shall keep my sabbaths and reverence my sanctuary: I am the LORD" (Lev. 19:30) and reiterated by the use of the term "slave" to refer to the people. In Hebrew the root has a dual meaning, "to serve" or "to worship."

Finally, Haggai and Zechariah 1–8 turned to practical concerns. Like Deutero-Isaiah, the prophets at the close of the sixth century understood that the time of judgment had passed. Living in the new era of Yahweh's rule required the reconstruction of the deity's sanctuary. Haggai proclaimed the message to rebuild, and Zechariah encouraged the people to continue their endeavors. In addition, Zechariah 1–8 contained a vision for the future like that of Ezekiel 40–48 and the Holiness Code. Proto-Zechariah showed how the community could reorganize itself and its ritual observance in the homeland.

The literature at the close of the templeless age marks the reversal of the disastrous events that took place when Jerusalem fell in 587 BCE. Priest and prophet together steered the nation on its future course.

Conclusion

In this short introduction I have argued that the period following the downfall of Judah is best spoken of as the templeless age. The centrality of worship in the literature commonly thought to stem from the time, the types of themes on which it drew, the continuation of the material culture to the end of the sixth century (at least in the Benjamin region), and the reassessment of religion that took place support a different designation than "the exile." This redefinition equally urges a reconsideration of the dates associated with the period. Rather than suggesting a closing date for a situation that never in fact ceased to exist, "templeless" clarifies a time frame—that epic period between the two temples. Between 587 and 515 BCE copious activity in the form of prayer, historiography, law, and prophecy created meaning out of the destruction that had taken place, as priests and prophets spoke on behalf of Yahweh, explaining the deity's behavior and declaring the renewal of divine presence and providence. In extending the era to the end of the sixth century, this study has been able to draw together the important contributions of Jeremiah, Ezekiel, and Deutero-Isaiah and view them alongside the prophetic activity of Haggai and Zechariah and the law of the Holiness Code. Each comes into clearer focus when viewed as part of the templeless age. Like the material culture, they exhibit greater continuity with what preceded them.

Grouping the literature of the templeless age according to overarching themes—immediate responses to disaster, weal and woe, and visions of renewal and restoration—rather than by biblical books throws into relief the different strands of thought generated by the fall of Jerusalem.

Prophets, priests, law, and prayer all provided channels for individuals and society to express their loss, frustration, even shock, and to move past raw emotions by firmly holding on to divine promises. I now will consider the strategies they employed.

Communication. The liturgy gave expression to immediate reactions, allowing the nation to work through its grief. Through prayer (in the Psalms and Lamentations) a grief-stricken nation approached its deity in its suffering. The laments exhibit accusations of, but also trust in, Yahweh. Each heartfelt prayer sought Yahweh's presence and powerful intervention, sometimes just the deity's attention, in the recognition that only a divine response could overturn such a humiliating present. The pitiful cries and angry curses exemplify faithful approach to the divine throne and communication with the deity. Through it all, the Judahites expressed a fundamental belief in a divine power above and beyond human might.

Creativity. The literature of the templeless age exhibits great creativity and religious imagination. Traditions that circulated separately before the downfall of the kingdom were welded together to create new meaning. The psalmists joined traditions from the realm of myth and history in order to express the depth of what was lost and to urge its renewal. The intertwining of elements further insisted on the universal power of Yahweh. Deutero-Isaiah would also link mythological and election traditions in his prophecy, but as a means of creating a sense of Yahweh's purposes to save and of the inbreaking of divine action in the world.

Memory. In the aftermath of disaster, historians considered the past in order to assess what went wrong. For ancient Israel, social ills and covenant disloyalty led to the downfall of the kingdom. A community remembered a sorrowful history in order to start anew through critical awareness of human and divine actions. Significantly, the historical account functioned also as a confession of sin. In the downfall of the nation, the people themselves had been culpable. The collapse of the kingdom(s) was taken as an opportunity to reflect on and learn from previous mistakes. Honestly owning up to human error created the opportunity for divine restoration, reconciliation, and relationality. It is not surprising, then, that remembrance of Yahweh's past actions on behalf of Judah were called to mind, not simply to dwell on a past that saw the fruition of divine promises, but to remind the deity of ongoing responsibility to a particular people.

Adaptation. The prophetic traditions of the period reveal how the word of the deity could be understood over time and in different circumstances. Through the editing and updating of traditions, Yahwists honored the divine word mediated by the prophets. Moreover, faithful communities added to prophecies in order to understand Yahweh's words in a new situation. What better way to attest to the power of a deity involved with a people in history? Even the prophet Deutero-Isaiah understood his mission differently over time. Called originally to speak to Jacob/Israel, he expanded his message to include the deity's plans for the nations. By so doing, he continued to work out the meaning of Yahweh's purposes for the people of ancient Israel, for the exiles, and for himself.

Inheritance. Closely related to the above, inheritance suggests that later generations drew upon past traditions. The words of the law and the prophets did not remain stagnant, but instead formed the basis of a new word in an altered situation. As the events of history changed the physical and symbolic landscape, the mediation of the divine word shifted to account for radically different events. The Holiness Code drew on legal material from before the templeless age and recast it as a means of signaling the availability of a renewed relationship with Yahweh. Similarly, the prophecies of Jeremiah and Ezekiel drew attention to the fulfillment of prophetic conceptions of the Day of the LORD. Even the words of Haggai and Zechariah drew on earlier traditions to speak a new word. Their words circulated in a prophetic milieu that provided fresh vision over time. The collapse of Judah taught that Yahweh's word was flexible and remained fresh in dramatically altered circumstances. Scriptural authority stemmed from its ability to convey a sense of Yahweh in and through historical changes.

Inclusion. Another feature of the literature of this period is the ease with which a variety of perspectives are held together. Two different understandings of how to respond to suffering are laid alongside each other. Lady Jerusalem and the objective eyewitness in Lamentations shouted of loss and the need to vocalize a painful present; in contrast, the Suffering Servant of Deutero-Isaiah and the strong man of Lamentations 3 exemplified silent submission to fate and the redemptive value of suffering. The Suffering Servant and Lady Jerusalem in some respects represent the different communities that experienced the disaster. Isaiah 49–55 and Lamentations spoke equally to the repatriates and the non-repatriates. Furthermore, the prophets Haggai and Zechariah spoke to a community that had been divided by distance in a way that brought them together in a singularity of purpose. The literature exemplifies this inclusive outlook by democratizing promises originally made to the king (as in Deutero-Isaiah) and by regarding the people and the priests as equals (as in the Holiness Code). Rather than being the occasion for division and acrimony, the collapse of Judah, followed by the deportation and flight of its citizenry, led to innovative strategies to hold the community and their diverse experiences together.

EXILE—THEN AND NOW

The destruction of the temple and Jerusalem shattered two physical symbols of the deity's abiding presence in ancient Israel. The sanctuary represented the dwelling place of the deity, and the royal palace (neighboring the sanctuary) signified Yahweh's choice of a human representative. The destruction of the capital city of Judah included the removal not only of significant structures that provided a sense of identity, but also of the political, religious, and social leaders of the community.

When considering the result of the devastating Neo-Babylonian campaign in this way, the use of the term "exile" makes sense. Exile conveys the captivity of the nation's identity and authority. Recent work on the concept of exile has explored its use as a motif for faithful living in modern society (Brueggemann 1997; Smith-Christopher 2002). The adoption of the perspective of exile raises awareness of the limits of societal structures such as consumerism and political/military systems. Moreover, understanding oneself as in exile creates a critical distance that affords opportunities to critique aspects of culture that fail to reflect true humanity. There is a particularism in the exilic point of view that suggests being called out and redeemed, and encourages a critique of the surrounding culture.

In confronting the challenge of living in a foreign environment, the exilic response modeled the means to live faithfully away from the homeland and what is familiar. The Judahites deported to Babylon settled into their communities, learned about a new culture, and reconsidered their own. Babylon was a cosmopolitan society with impressive visual symbols of the empire and its gods. The Ishtar gate in the Pergamon Museum in Berlin provides a vivid example of the types of iconography that confronted the exiles. The Babylonians created colorful glazed bricks that had raised figures impressed upon them. They covered the walls of the buildings at the entrance into the city and on many thoroughfares. In addition, Babylon was famed for its Hanging Gardens, which added a lush green atmosphere to the city. It was an impressive place. Rather than be lured by a more sophisticated and cosmopolitan culture, Judahites took stock and reassessed their identity and traditions. They understood the allure of Babylon as a challenge to be confronted.

Their thoughts led to a new expression of their identity and the development of observances aimed at physically symbolizing an awareness of lives shaped by and dedicated to their own god, Yahweh. The development of traditions as a confessional act led to principles adopted in Judaism. In responding to the challenge of culture in this way, the exiles adopted a nonviolent reaction to difference and change. Babylon provided the opportunity to create new expressions of identity. The biblical tradition of this time suggests something more nuanced than a complete rejection of an alien and provocative culture and can surely teach the current generation something about ways to express difference.

Daniel Smith-Christopher has worked out a biblical theology of exile by taking into account the serious situation confronting Judahites forcibly deported to Babylon and living in Diaspora under an imperial ruler. From observations of exilic responses, he urges the adoption of diaspora existence for modern Christians. A helpful introduction to his view is provided in his statement that "Christian strategies seek, like Daniel and Tobit, to assert nonviolently alternative strategies for human existence in the world that are lived out in conscious nonconformity to the world and its various value systems" while acknowledging that "the precise terms of a diasporic Christianity must be revisited in each different geographical location" (2002: 194). Through his work on creating a biblical theology out of the exilic experience of the sixth century BCE, Smith-Christopher has provided a means to challenge cultural standards and models that do not express the sanctity of humanity. It is a powerful expression of how biblical texts far removed in time can have meaning for communities today.

Diaspora as a concept may also say something about the formation of the Hebrew Bible. Robert Carroll has studied the use of the tropes of disaster, exile, and restoration in the prophetic literature (1997). The focus of Amos is almost exclusively on disaster. But most of the other prophets in the book of the Twelve and Isaiah, Jeremiah, and Ezekiel concentrate on exile and restoration. Through his examination, Carroll has astutely observed that the Hebrew Bible itself is shaped by the tropes exile and return. According to the sequence of books in the Hebrew Bible, the biblical story begins with the expulsion of Adam and Eve from the garden of Eden and ends with Cyrus's command to the deported Judahites to return and rebuild Jerusalem (2 Chr. 36:22–23). Further concentration by scholars on the question of how the Hebrew Bible took shape must pay attention to how the reality of Diaspora influenced the biblical writers' consciousness.

THE "TEMPLELESS" PERSPECTIVE

Even though Smith-Christopher and Carroll speak of diaspora, both show in their studies how an exilic viewpoint maintains an equally significant emphasis on homecoming. To be in exile is to be separated from what is perceived as authentic living. Given that there was not a complete societal and political break with monarchic Judah, the question arises as to how the perspective of the population that remained in the land might influence or adjust awareness of the events and thought of the period. What insights can be afforded by a view that concentrates on being "templeless" rather than the urge to return? If exile generates greater awareness of a person of faith as separated from prevailing cultural standards and values, what insight does a "templeless" perspective hold?

It is difficult to convey a sense of what the temple meant in the ancient world. The Jerusalem sanctuary was understood to be where the heavenly and the earthly realms intersected. More than that, it was the place of Yahweh's throne—where the deity abided among a chosen people, from which divine presence and protection were mediated, and in which a community celebrated and honored its God in great pilgrimage festivals. In response to the collapse of one of the chief physical symbols of Yahweh's rule, the templeless literature concentrated on two foci: reassessments of Yahweh and reappraisals of the human person. The thought of the period showed the intimate connection between the deity and a people, with the people being understood as one community. Just as the prophecies of Haggai and Zechariah urged a common goal to a society welded from two very different circumstances (the remnant in the homeland and the repatriates from Babylon, presumably including returned refugees, as well), the literary deposit exhibits variety and is inclusive of different points of view. In contrast to the turn to the particular in "exile," "templeless" stresses the power of creative strategies to grapple with the inexplicability of the deity and to support a unified identity.

As well as taking account of those who remained or returned, scholars are increasingly aware of the importance of the perspective of those who continued to live in the Diaspora (e.g., D. Boyarin and J. Boyarin 1993). Rather than constantly hoping for return to a homeland, Diaspora consciousness invites the employment of strategies to live faithfully in a foreign environment, with the recognition that life outside the land was as valuable as that within it. A number of the refugees and deportees never returned to Judah. Instead, they engaged fully in the communities in which they lived, made contracts, participated in local governance, prayed for the empire, and intermarried—all as faithful citizens of another worldview. The communities in Diaspora learned how to coexist peacefully away from their homeland by educating themselves about a new culture and developing strategies that allowed them to live as persons of faith in an environment with different cultural and religious norms.

The literature of the templeless age thus demonstrates an acceptance of variety and difference. The situation without the temple united a population in the far reaches of the world—refugees in Egypt and elsewhere, a population in the homeland, and deportees in Babylon. The texts they produced witness to a range of responses, all held to be faithful, all Scripture. If "the exile" creates a sense of particularity and difference, "templeless" highlights that which is held in common, and suggests creative, unifying strategies for communities of faith today.

Reference List

INTRODUCTION

Introductions to the Literature, History, and Thought of the Period

Ackroyd, P. R. 1970. *Israel under Babylon and Persia.* Oxford: Oxford University Press.

————. 1994. *Exile and Restoration.* Repr., London: XPress Reprints.

Albertz, R. 2003. *Israel in Exile: An Introduction to the History and Literature of the Sixth Century BCE.* Studies in Biblical Literature 3. Atlanta: SBL.

Foster, R. S. 1970. *The Restoration of Israel: A Study in Exile and Return.* London: Darton, Longman, & Todd.

Klein, R. W. 2002. *Israel in Exile: A Theological Interpretation.* Repr., Mifflintown, PA: Sigler Press.

Newsome, J. D. 1979. *By the Waters of Babylon: An Introduction to the History and Theology of Exile.* Edinburgh: T. & T. Clark.

Noth, M. 1966. The Jerusalm Catastrophe of 587 B.C., and Its Significance for Israel. In *The Laws of the Pentateuch and Other Essays,* 260–80. Edinburgh: Oliver & Boyd.

Smith-Christopher, D. L. 1989. *The Religion of the Landless: The Social Context of the Babylonian Exile.* Bloomington, IN: Meyer-Stone Books.

On Religious Belief

Albrektson, B. 1967. *History and the Gods: An Essay on the Idea of Historical Events as Divine Manifestations in the Ancient Near East and in Israel.* ConBOT 1. Lund: Gleerup.

Barton, J. 1995. Wellhausen's Prolegomena to the History of Israel: Influence and Effects. In *Text and Experience: Toward a Cultural Exegesis of the Bible*, ed. D. L. Smith-Christopher, 316–29. BS 35. Sheffield: Sheffield Academic Press.

Becking, B. 1999. Continuity and Discontinuity after the Exile: Some Introductory Remarks. In *The Crisis of Israelite Religion*, ed. B. Becking and M. C. A. Korpel, 1–8.

Becking, B., and M. C. A. Korpel, eds. 1999. *The Crisis of Israelite Religion: Transformation of Religious Tradition in Exilic and Post-Exilic Times.* OtSt 42. Leiden: Brill.

Gnuse, R. K. 1997. *No Other Gods: Emergent Monotheism in Israel.* JSOTSup 241. Sheffield: Sheffield Academic Press.

Knight, D. A., ed. 1983. Julius Wellhausen and His *Prolegomena to the History of Israel. Semeia* 25. This journal contains a helpful collection of articles on Wellhausen's contribution to the understanding of Israelite religion.

Lang, B. 1983. *Monotheism and the Prophetic Minority: An Essay in Biblical History and Sociology.* The Social World of Biblical Antiquity 1. Sheffield: Almond.

Saggs, H. W. F. 1978. *The Encounter with the Divine in Mesopotamia and Israel.* Jordan Lectures in Comparative Religion 12. London: Athlone Press.

Smith, M. 1987. *Palestinian Parties and Politics that Shaped the Old Testament.* Repr., London: SCM Press.

Wellhausen, J. 1957. *Prolegomena to the History of Israel.* Repr., New York: Meridian.

On the Diaspora and Its Importance Well beyond the "Exile"

Coggins, R. J. 1989. The Origins of the Jewish Diaspora. In *The World of Ancient Israel: Sociological, Anthropological and Political Perspectives*, ed. R. E. Clements, 163–81. Cambridge: Cambridge University Press.

Knibb, M. A. 1976. The Exile in the Literature of the Intertestamental Period. *HeyJ* 17:253–72.

Scott, J. M., ed. 1997. *Exile: Old Testament, Jewish, and Christian Conceptions.* JSJSup 56. Leiden: Brill.

On the Use of the Term "Exile" and the Adoption of its Perspective

Barstad, H. 1996. *The Myth of the Empty Land: A Study in the History and Archaeology of Judah during the "Exilic" Period.* SO 28. Oslo: Scandinavian University Press.

Carroll R. P 1992. The Myth of the Empty Land. In *Ideological Criticism of Biblical Texts*, ed. D. Jobling and T. Pippin, 79–93. Semeia 59. Atlanta: Scholars Press.

Grabbe, L. L., ed. 1998. *Leading Captivity Captive: "The Exile" as History and Ideology.* JSOTSup 278 and ESHM 2. Sheffield: Sheffield Academic Press.

Important Work in Languages Other than English

Janssen, E. 1956. *Juda in der Exilszeit: Ein Beitrag zur Entstehung des Judentums.* Göttingen: Vandenhoeck & Ruprecht.

CHAPTER ONE

Albertz, R. 2003. *Israel in Exile: An Introduction to the History and Literature of the Sixth Century BCE.* Studies in Biblical Literature 3. Atlanta: SBL.

Barstad, H. 1996. *The Myth of the Empty Land: A Study in the History and Archaeology of Judah during the "Exilic" Period.* SO 28. Oslo: Scandinavian University Press.

———. 1998. The Strange Fear of the Bible: Some Reflections on the "Bibliophobia" in Recent Ancient Israelite Historiography. In *Leading Captivity Captive*, ed. L. L. Grabbe, 120–27.

Bedford, P. R. 2001. *Temple Reconstruction in Early Achaemenid Judah.* JSJSup 65. Leiden: Brill.

Blenkinsopp, J. 2002a. The Age of Exile. In *The Biblical World*, ed. J. Barton, 416–39. London and New York: Routledge.

———. 2002b. There Was No Gap. *BAR* 28/3:36–38, 59.

Clements, R. E. 1965. *God and Temple: The Presence of God in Israel's Worship.* Oxford: Basil Blackwell.

Coogan, M. D. 1974. Life in the Diaspora: Jews at Nippur in the Fifth Century B.C. *BA* 37:6–12.

Davies, P. R. 1995. *In Search of "Ancient Israel."* JSOTSup 148. 2nd ed., Sheffield: Sheffield Academic Press.

Day, J. 1986. Asherah in the Hebrew Bible and Northwest Semitic Literature. *JBL* 105: 385–408.

———. 2000. *Yahweh and the Gods and Goddesses of Canaan.* JSOTSup 265. Sheffield: Sheffield Academic Press.

Edelman, D. V., ed. 1991. *The Fabric of History: Text, Artifact and Israel's Past.* JSOTSup 127. Sheffield: Sheffield Academic Press.

———. 2005. *The Origins of the "Second Temple": Persian Imperial Policy and the Rebuilding of Jerusalem.* London: Equinox.

Fried, L. S. 2006. The 'am ha'ares in Ezra 4:4 and Persian Imperial Administration. In *Judah and the Judeans in the Persian Period*, ed. O. Lipschits and M. Oeming, 123–45.

Grabbe, L. L., ed. 1998. *Leading Captivity Captive: "The Exile" as History and Ideology.* JSOTSup 278 and ESHM 2. Sheffield: Sheffield Academic Press.

Glassner, J.-J. 2004. *Mesopotamian Chronicles.* Writings from the Ancient World 19. Atlanta: SBL.

Hallo, W. W., ed. 2000. *Context of Scripture,* vol. 3, *Archival Documents from the Biblical World.* Leiden: Brill.

Hoffman, Y. 2003. The Fasts in the Book of Zechariah and the Fashioning of National Remembrance. In O. Lipschits and J. Blenkinsopp, *Judah and the Judeans in the Neo-Babylonian Period,* 169–218.

Hoglund, K. G. 1991. The Achemenid Context. In *Second Temple Studies,* vol. 1, *Persian Period,* ed. P. R. Davies. JSOTSup 117. Sheffield: JSOT Press.

———. 1992. *Achaemenid Imperial Administration in Syria-Palestine and the Missions of Ezra and Nehemiah.* SBLDS 125. Atlanta: Scholars Press.

Joannès, F., and A. Lemaire. 1999. Trois tablettes cunéiformes à l'onomastique ouest-sémitique. *Transeuphratène* 17:17–33.

Jones, D. 1963. The Cessation of Sacrifice after the Destruction of the Temple in 586 B.C. *JTS,* n.s., 14:12–31.

Kuhrt, A. 1983. The Cyrus Cylinder and Achaemenid Imperial Policy. *JSOT* 25:83–97.

———. 1995. *The Ancient Near East c. 3000–330 B.C.,* vol. 2. Routledge History of the Ancient World. London and New York: Routledge.

Lipschits, O. 1998. Nebuchadnezzar's Policy in "Hattu Land" and the Fate of the Kingdom of Judah. *UF* 30:467–87.

———. 1999. The History of the Benjamin Region under Babylonian Rule. *Tel Aviv* 26 (1999): 155–90.

———. 2001. Judah, Jerusalem and the Temple 586–539 B.C. *Transeuphratène* 22:129–42.

———. 2005. *The Fall and Rise of Jerusalem.* Winona Lake, IN: Eisenbrauns.

Lipschits, O., and J. Blenkinsopp, eds. 2003. *Judah and the Judeans in the Neo-Babylonian Period.* Winona Lake, IN: Eisenbrauns.

Lipschits, O., and M. Oeming, eds. 2006. *Judah and the Judeans in the Persian Period.* Winona Lake, IN: Eisenbrauns.

Long, V., ed. 1999. *Israel's Past in Present Research: Essays on Ancient Israelite Historiography.* SBTS 7. Winona Lake, IN: Eisenbrauns.

Malamat, A. 1950. The Last Wars of the Kingdom of Judah. *JNES* 9:218–27.

———. 1968. The Last Kings of Judah and the Fall of Jerusalem. *IEJ* 18:137–56.

———. 1975. The Twilight of Judah: In the Egyptian-Babylonian Maelstrom. In *Congress Volume, 1974,* 123–45. VTSup 28. Leiden: Brill.

———. 1999. Caught between the Great Powers: Judah Chooses a Side . . . and Loses. *BAR* 25/4:34–41.

Middlemas, J. 2005. *The Troubles of Templeless Judah.* Oxford Theological Monographs. Oxford: Oxford University Press.

Miller, J. M. 1991. Is It Possible to Write a History of Israel without Relying on the Hebrew Bible? In *The Fabric of History*, ed. D. V. Edelman, 93–102.

Miller, J. M., and J. H. Hayes. 2006. *A History of Ancient Israel and Judah.* 2nd ed., Louisville, KY: Westminster John Knox Press.

Oded, B. 1979. *Mass Deportations and Deportees in the Neo-Assyrian Empire.* Wiesbaden: Reichert.

Pearce, L. E. 2006. New Evidence for Judeans in Babylonia. In *Judah and the Judeans in the Persian Period*, ed. O. Lipschits and M. Oeming, 399–411.

Porten, B. 1968. *Archives from Elephantine: The Life of an Ancient Jewish Military Colony.* Berkeley: University of California Press.

———. 1996. *The Elephantine Papyri in English: Three Millennia of Cross-Cultural Continuity and Change.* Leiden: Brill.

———. 2003. Settlement of the Jews at Elephantine and the Arameans at Syene. In *Judah and the Judeans in the Neo-Babylonian Period*, ed. O. Lipschits and J. Blenkinsopp, 451–70.

Seitz, Christopher R. 1989. *Theology in Conflict: Reactions to the Exile in the Book of Jeremiah.* BZAW 176. Berlin: de Gruyter.

Smith(-Christopher), D. L. 1989. *The Religion of the Landless: The Social Context of the Babylonian Exile.* Bloomington, IN: Meyer-Stone Books.

———. 2002. *A Biblical Theology of Exile.* OBT; Minneapolis: Fortress Press.

Smith, M. 1975. The Veracity of Ezekiel, the Sins of Manasseh, and Jeremiah 44:18. *ZAW* 87:11–16.

Stager, L. E. 1996a. Ashkelon and the Archaeology of Destruction: Kislev 604 B.C.E. *ErIsr* 25:61*–74*.

————. 1996b. The Fury of Babylon: The Archaeology of Destruction. *BAR* 22/1:56–69, 76–77.

Stern, E. 2000. The Babylonian Gap. *BAR* 26/6:45–51.

————. 2001. *Archaeology in the Land of the Bible*, vol. 2, *The Assyrian, Babylonian, and Persian Periods 732–332 B.C.E.* New York: Doubleday.

————. 2002. Yes, There Was. *BAR* 28/3:39, 55.

————. 2004. The Babylonian Gap: The Archaeological Reality. *JSOT* 28:273–77.

Vanderhooft, D. S. 1999. *The Neo-Babylonian Empire and Babylon in the Latter Prophets.* HSM 59. Atlanta: Scholars Press.

————. 2003. Babylonian Strategies of Imperial Control in the West: Royal Practice and Rhetoric. In *Judah and the Judeans in the Neo-Babylonian Period,* ed. O. Lipschits and M. Blenkinsopp, 235–62.

Zorn, J. R. 1997. Mizpah: Newly Discovered Stratum Reveals Judah's Other Capital. *BAR* 23/5:29–38, 66.

————. 2003. Tell en-Nasbeh and the Problem of the Material Culture of the Sixth Century. In *Judah and the Judeans in the Neo-Babylonian Period,* ed. O. Lipschits and M. Blenkinsopp, 413–47.

CHAPTER TWO

General

Clements, R. E. 1965. *God and Temple: The Presence of God in Israel's Worship.* Philadelphia: Fortress Press.

Day, J. 1985. *God's Conflict with the Dragon and the Sea: Echoes of a Canaanite Myth in the Old Testament.* COP 35. Cambridge: Cambridge University Press.

Mettinger, T. N. D. 1982. *The Dethronement of Sabaoth: Studies in Shem and Kabod Theology.* ConBOT 18. Lund: Gleerup.

Nicholson, E. 1998. *The Pentateuch in the Twentieth Century: The Legacy of Julius Wellhausen.* Oxford: Oxford University Press.

Whybray, R. N. 1995. *Introduction to the Pentateuch.* Grand Rapids: Eerdmans.

Biblical and Other Ancient Near Eastern Literature

Ackroyd, P. R. 1994. *Exile and Restoration.* Repr., London: XPress Reprints.

Anderson, G. A. 1991. *A Time to Mourn, a Time to Dance: The Expression of Grief and Joy in Israelite Religion.* University Park: Pennsylvania State University Press.

Coates, G. W. 1968. *Rebellion in the Wilderness*. Nashville: Abingdon Press.

Dobbs-Allsopp, F. W. 1993. *Weep, O Daughter of Zion: A Study of the City-Lament Genre in the Hebrew Bible*. BibOr 44. Rome: Pontifical Biblical Institute.

Ferris, P. W. 1992. *The Genre of Communal Lament in the Bible and Ancient Near East*. SBLDS; Atlanta: Scholars Press.

Hallo, W. W., ed. 1997. *The Context of Scripture*, vol. 1, *Canonical Compositions from the Biblical World*, 535–39. Leiden: Brill.

Herdner, A. 1963. *Corpus des Tablettes en cunéiformes alphaétiques*. Misson de Ras-Shamra. Paris: Geuthner.

Hoffman, Y. 2003. The Fasts in the Book of Zechariah and the Fashioning of National Remembrance. In O. Lipschits and J. Blenkinsopp, *Judah and the Judeans in the Neo-Babylonian Period*, 169–218.

Klein, J. 1997. Lamentation over the Destruction of Sumer and Ur. In *The Context of Scripture*, ed. W. W. Hallo, 1:535–39.

Longman, T. 1997. The Adad-Guppi Autobiography. In *The Context of Scripture*, ed. W. W. Hallo, 1:477–78.

Meyers, C. L., and E. M. Meyers. 1987. *Haggai, Zechariah 1–8*. AB 25B. New York: Doubleday.

Olyan, S. M. 2004. *Biblical Mourning: Ritual and Social Dimensions*. Oxford: Oxford University Press.

Pham, X. H. T. 1999. *Mourning in the Ancient Near East and the Hebrew Bible*. JSOTSup 302. Sheffield: Sheffield Academic Press.

Porten, B. 1968. *Archives from Elephantine: The Life of a Jewish Military Colony*. Berkeley: University of California Press.

———. 1996. *The Elephantine Papyri in English: Three Millennia of Cross-Cultural Continuity and Change*. DMOA 22. Leiden: Brill.

Westermann, C. 1981. *Praise and Lament in the Psalms*. Repr., Atlanta: John Knox Press.

On the Judahite Situation—General Themes

Blenkinsopp, J. 1998. The Judaean Priesthood during the Neo-Babylonian and Achaemenid Periods: A Hypothetical Reconstruction. *CBQ* 60:25–43.

———. 2002. The Age of the Exile. In *The Biblical World*, ed. J. Barton, 1:416–39. London and New York: Routledge.

———. 2003. Bethel in the Neo-Babylonian Period. In *Judah and the Judeans in the Neo-Babylonian Period*, ed. O. Lipschits and J. Blenkinsopp, 93–107.

Hayes, J. H. 1963. The Tradition of Zion's Inviolability. *JBL* 82:419–26.

Lipschits, O. 2001. Judah, Jerusalem and the Temple 586–539 B.C. *Transeuphratène* 22:129–42.

———. 2005. *The Fall and Rise of Jerusalem: Judah in the Neo-Babylonian Period.* Winona Lake, IN: Eisenbrauns.

Lipschits, O., and J. Blenkinsopp, eds. 2003. *Judah and the Judeans in the Neo-Babylonian Period.* Winona Lake, IN: Eisenbrauns.

Middlemas, J. 2005a. *The Troubles of Templeless Judah* (Oxford Theological Monographs; Oxford: Oxford University Press).

Lamentations

Berlin, A. 2002. *Lamentations.* OTL. Louisville, KY: Westminster John Knox Press.

Dobbs-Allsopp, F. W. 1997. Tragedy, Tradition, and Theology in the Book of Lamentations. *JSOT* 74:29–60.

———. 2002. *Lamentations.* Interpretation. Louisville, KY: Westminster John Knox Press.

Lee, N. C. 2002. *The Singers of Lamentations: Cities under Siege, from Ur to Jerusalem to Sarajevo.* BIS 60. Leiden: Brill.

Linafelt, T. 2000a. Zion's Cause: The Presentation of Pain in the Book of Lamentations. In *Strange Fire: Reading the Bible after the Holocaust,* ed. T. Linafelt, 267–79. BS 71. Sheffield: Sheffield Academic Press.

———. 2000b. *Surviving Lamentations: Catastrophe, Lament, and Protest in the Afterlife of a Biblical Book.* Chicago: University of Chicago Press.

Middlemas, J. 2004. The Violent Storm in Lamentations. *JSOT* 29/1: 81–97.

———. 2006. Did Second Isaiah Write Lamentations 3? *VT* LVI/4:505–25.

Provan, I. 1991. *Lamentations.* NCB. London: Marshall Pickering.

von Rad, G. 1966. Faith Reckoned as Righteousness. In *The Problem of the Hexateuch and Other Essays,* 125–30. Edinburgh: Oliver & Boyd. On Psalm 106 and the book of Romans.

Reimer, D. J. 2002. Good Grief? A Psychological Reading of Lamentations. *ZAW* 114:542–59.

Westermann, C. 1994. *Lamentations: Issues and Interpretation.* Edinburgh: T. & T. Clark.

Willey, P. T. 1997. *Remember the Former Things: The Recollection of Previous Texts in Second Isaiah.* Atlanta: Scholars Press.

Williamson, H. G. M. 1990. Laments at the Destroyed Temple. *BRev* 4/4:12–17, 44.

————. 2004. Structure and Historiography in Nehemiah 9. In *Studies in Persian Period History and Historiography*, 282–93. FAT 38. Tübingen: Mohr Siebeck.

Psalms

Allen, L. C. 2002. *Psalms 101–50.* WBC 21. Repr., Nashville: Thomas Nelson.

Broyles, C. C. 1989. *The Conflict of Faith and Experience in the Psalms: A Form Critical and Theological Study.* JSOTSup 52. Sheffield: JSOT Press.

Brueggemann, W. 1995. *The Psalms and the Life of Faith.* Minneapolis: Fortress Press.

Clifford, R. J. 1980. Psalm 89: A Lament over the Davidic Ruler's Continued Failure. *HTR* 73:35–47.

Craigie, P. C. 2004. *Psalms 1–50.* WBC 19. Repr., Nashville: Thomas Nelson.

Day, J. 1990. *Psalms.* OTG. Sheffield: JSOT Press.

Gunkel, H. 1998. *Introduction to the Psalms: The Genres of the Religious Lyric of Israel,* completed by J. Begrich. Macon, GA: Mercer University Press.

Heim, K. M. 1998. The (God-)Forsaken King in Psalm 89: A Historical and Intertextual Enquiry. In *King and Messiah in Israel and the Ancient Near East,* ed. J. Day, 296–322. JSOTSup 270. Sheffield: JSOT Press.

Mitchell, M. C. 2005. Genre Disputes and Communal Accusatory Laments: Reflections on the Genre of Psalm lxxxix. *VT* 55:511–27.

Mowinckel, S. 1962. *The Psalms in Israel's Worship,* 2 vols. Eng. trans. Oxford: Basil Blackwell.

Tate, M. E. 1990. *Psalms 51–100.* WBC 20. Dallas: Word Books.

Watson, R. S. 2005. *Chaos Uncreated: A Reassessment of the Theme of "Chaos" in the Hebrew Bible.* BZAW 341. Berlin: Walter de Gruyter.

Trito–Isaiah

Blenkinsopp, J. 2003. *Isaiah 56–66.* AB 19B. New York: Doubleday.

Middlemas, J. 2005b. Divine Reversal and the Role of the Temple in Trito-Isaiah. In *Temple and Worship in Biblical Israel,* ed. J. Day, 164–87. Library of Hebrew Bible/Old Testament Studies 422. London: T. & T. Clark.

Smith, P. A. 1995. *Rhetoric and Redaction in Trito-Isaiah: The Structure, Growth, and Authorship of Isaiah 56–66.* VTSup 62. Leiden: Brill.

Westermann, C. 1969. *Isaiah 40–66.* OTL. London: SCM Press.

Williamson, H. G. M 1990. Isaiah 63:7–64:11: Exilic Lament or Post-Exilic Protest? *ZAW* 102:48–58.

Zechariah 1–8

Edelman, D. V. 2005. *The Origins of the "Second Temple": Persian Imperial Policy and the Rebuilding of Jerusalem.* London: Equinox.

Hyatt, J. P. 1937. A Neo-Babylonian Parallel to Bethel-sar-Eser, Zech 7:2. *JBL* 56:387–94.

Important Contributions in Languages Other than English

Berges, U. 2004. Kann Zion männlich sein?—Klgl 3 als "literarisches Drama" und "Nachexilische Problemdichtung." In *"Basel und Bibel": Collected Communications to the XVIIth Congress of the International Organization for the Study of the Old Testament,* ed. M. Augustin and H. M. Niemann, 235–46. Frankfurt am Main: Peter Lang.

Dumortier, J.-B. 1972. Un rituel d'intronisation: le Ps lxxxix 2–38. *VT* 22:176–96.

Jahnow, H. 1923. Das Hebräische Leichenlied im Rahmen der Völkerdichtung. *BZAW* 36. Giessen: Alfred Töpelmann.

Wellhausen, J. 1898. *Die Kleinen Propheten.* 3rd ed., Berlin: G. Reimer.

CHAPTER THREE

The Deuteronomistic History

Clements, R. E. 1965. *God and Temple: The Presence of God in Israel's Worship.* Oxford: Basil Blackwell.

Cross, F. M. 1973. *Canaanite Myth and Hebrew Epic: Essays in the History of the Religion of Israel,* 274–89. Cambridge, MA: Harvard University Press.

Fretheim, T. E. 1983. *Deuteronomistic History.* Nashville: Abingdon Press.

Gerbrandt, G. E. 1986. *Kingship according to the Deuteronomistic History.* SBLDS 87. Atlanta: Scholars Press.

Hayes, J. H. 1963. Tradition of Zion's Inviolability. *JBL* 82:419–26.

Lowery, R. H. 1991. *The Reforming Kings.* JSOTSup 120. Sheffield: JSOT Press.

McCarthy, D. J. 1965. 2 Samuel 7 and the Structure of the Deuteronomistic History. *JBL* 84:131–38.

McKenzie, S. L., and M. P. Graham, eds. 1994. *The History of Israel's Traditions: The Heritage of Martin Noth.* JSOTSup 182. Sheffield: Sheffield Academic Press.

Mayes, A. D. H. 1983. *The Story of Israel between Settlement and Exile: A Redactional Study of the Deuteronomistic History.* London: SCM Press.

———. 1999. The Deuteronomistic History and the Theology of the Old Testament. *JSOT* 82:57–82.

Mettinger, T. N. D. 1982. *The Dethronement of Sabaoth: Studies in the Shem and Kabod Theologies.* ConBOT 18. Lund: Gleerup.

Murray, D. F. 2001. Of All the Years the Hopes—or Fears? Jehoiachin in Babylon. *JBL* 120:245–65.

Nelson, R. D. 1981. *The Double Redaction of the Deuteronomistic History.* JSOTSup 18. Sheffield: JSOT Press.

Noth, M. 1981. *The Deuteronomistic History,* Eng. trans. JSOTSup 15. Sheffield: JSOT Press.

O'Brien, M. A. 1989. *The Deuteronomistic History Hypothesis: A Reassessment.* OBO 92. Freiburg: Universitätsverlag.

von Rad, G. 1966. The Deuteronomic Theology of History in I and II Kings. In *The Problem of the Hexateuch and Other Essays,* 281–307. Edinburgh: Oliver & Boyd.

Stavrakopoulou, F. 2004. *King Manasseh and Child Sacrifice: Biblical Distortions of Historical Realities.* BZAW 338. Berlin and New York: Walter de Gruyter.

Wolff, H. W. 1975. The Kerygma of the Deuteronomistic Historian. In *The Vitality of Old Testament Traditions,* ed. W. Brueggemann and H. W. Wolff, 83–100. Atlanta: John Knox Press.

Important Contributions in Languages Other than English

Dietrich, W. 1972. *Prophetie und Geschichte: Eine Redaktionsgeschictliche Untersuchung zum deuteronomistischen Geschichtswerk.* FRLANT 108. Göttingen: Vandenhoeck & Ruprecht.

Janssen, E. 1956. *Juda in der Exilszeit: Ein Beitrag zur Entstehung des Judentums.* Göttingen: Vandenhoeck & Ruprecht.

Smend, R. 1971. Das Gesetz und die Völker: Ein Betrag zur deuteronomistischen Redaktionsgeschichte. In *Probleme biblischer Theologie: Gerhard von Rad zum 70. Geburtstag,* ed. H. W. Wolff, 494–509. (Munich: C. Kaiser.

Westermann, C. 1994. *Die Geschictsbücher des Alten Testaments: Gab es ein deuteronomistisches Geschictswerk?* Gütersloh: C. Kaiser.

CHAPTER FOUR

General

Albertz, R. 2003. *Israel in Exile: An Introduction to the History and Literature of the Sixth Century BCE.* Studies in Biblical Literature 3. Atlanta: SBL.

Blenksinsopp, J. 1996. *A History of Prophecy in Israel.* Rev. and enlarged, Louisville, KY: Westminster John Knox Press.

Blumenthal, D. R. 1993. *Facing the Abusing God: A Theology of Protest.* Louisville, KY: Westminster/John Knox Press.

Childs, B. 1979. *Introduction to the Old Testament as Scripture.* Philadelphia: Fortress Press.

Clements, R. E. 1965. *God and Temple: The Presence of God in Israel's Worship.* Oxford: Basil Blackwell.

Coates, G. W. 1968. *Rebellion in the Wilderness: The Murmuring Motif in the Wilderness Traditions of the Old Testament.* Nashville: Abingdon Press.

Coggins, R. R., A. Phillips, and M. Knibb, eds. 1982. *Israel's Prophetic Tradition: Essays in Honour of Peter Ackroyd.* Cambridge: Cambridge University Press.

Collins, J. J. 1984. *Daniel, with an Introduction to Apocalyptic Literature.* Grand Rapids: Eerdmans.

Cook, S. L. 1995. *Prophecy and Apocalypticism: The Postexilic Setting.* Minneapolis: Ausburg Fortress.

Grabbe, L. L. 1995. *Priests, Prophets, Diviners, Sages: A Socio-Historical Study of Religious Specialists in Ancient Israel.* Valley Forge, PA: Trinity Press, Intl.

Habel, N. 1965. The Form and Significance of the Call Narratives. *ZAW* 77:297–323.

Hanson, P. D. 1985. Apocalyptic Literature. In *The Hebrew Bible and Its Modern Interpreters,* ed. D. A. Knight and G. M. Tucker, 465–88. Philadelphia: Fortress Press.

Klein, R. W. 2002. *Israel in Exile: A Theological Interpretation.* Repr., Mifflintown, PA: Sigler Press.

Knibb, M. 1982. Prophecy and the Emergence of Jewish Apocalypses. In *Israel's Prophetic Tradition,* ed. R. Coggins et al., 155–80. Cambridge: Cambridge University Press.

Lipschits, O. 2005. *The Fall and Rise of Jerusalem.* Winona Lake, IN: Eisenbrauns.

Mason, R. 1982. The Prophets of the Restoration. In *Israel's Prophetic Tradition,* ed. R. Coggins et al., 137–54.

Mays, J. L., and P. J. Achtemeier, eds. 1987. *Interpreting the Prophets.* Philadelphia: Fortress Press.

McConville, J. G. 1993. *Grace in the End: A Study in Deuteronomic Theology.* Studies in Old Testament Biblical Theology. Grand Rapids: Zondervan.

Mettinger, T. N. D. 1982. *The Dethronement of Sabaoth: Studies in the Shem and Kabod Theologies.* ConBOT 18. Lund: Gleerup.

Newsome, J. D. 1984. *The Hebrew Prophets,* 124–38. Atlanta: John Knox.

Nissinen, M. 2003. *Prophets and Prophecy in the Ancient Near East.* Writings from the Ancient World 12. Atlanta: Society of Biblical Literature.

Orton, D. E., ed. 2000. *Prophecy in the Hebrew Bible: Selected Studies from Vetus Testamentum.* Brill's Reader in Biblical Studies 5. Leiden: Brill.

Petersen, D. L. 2002. *The Prophetic Literature: An Introduction.* Louisville, KY, and London: Westminster John Knox Press.

Römer, T. 2000. Is There a Deuteronomic Redaction in the Book of Jeremiah? In *Israel Constructs Its History: Deuteronomistic Historiography in Recent Research,* ed. A. de Pury, T. Römer, and J-D. Macchi, 399–421. JSOTSup 306. Sheffield: Sheffield Academic Press.

Sawyer, J. F. A. 1993. *Prophecy and the Biblical Prophets.* Rev. ed., Oxford: Oxford University Press.

Wilson, R. R. 1980. *Prophecy and Society in Ancient Israel.* Philadelphia: Fortress Press.

Vanderkam, J. 1998. Apocalyptic Literature. In *The Cambridge Companion to Biblical Interpretation,* ed. J. Barton, 305–22. Cambridge: Cambridge University Press.

Zimmerli, W. 1978. *Old Testament Theology in Outline.* Edinburgh: T. & T. Clark.

Amos

Coote, R. B. 1981. *Amos among the Prophets: Composition and Theology.* Philadelphia: Fortress Press.

Williamson, H. G. M. 1995. The Prophet and the Plumb-line: A Redaction Critical Study of Amos 7. In *The Place is Too Small for Us,* ed. R. P. Gordon, 435–77. Winona Lake, IN: Eisenbrauns.

Wolff, H. W. 1977. *Joel and Amos.* Hermeneia. Philadelphia: Fortress Press.

Ezekiel

Allen, L. C. 1994. *Ezekiel 1–19.* WBC 28. Waco, TX: Word Books.

Blenkinsopp, J. 1990. *Ezekiel.* Interpretation. Louisville, KY: John Knox Press.

Brueggemann, W. 1992. *Hopeful Imagination. Prophetic Voices in Exile.* London: SCM Press.

Clements, R. E. 1982. The Ezekiel Tradition: Prophecy in a Time of Crisis. In *Israel's Prophetic Tradition,* ed. R. Coggins et al., 119–36.

Darr, K. P. 1992. Ezekiel's Justification of God: Troubling Texts. *JSOT* 55:97–117.

Fishbane, M. 1987. Sin and Judgment in the Prophecies of Ezekiel. In *Interpreting the Prophets*, ed. J. L. Mays and P. J. Achtemeier, 170–87.

Greenberg, M. 1983. *Ezekiel 1–20*. AB 22. New York: Doubleday.

———. 1997. *Ezekiel 21–37*. AB 22A. New York: Doubleday.

Joyce, P. M. 1989. *Divine Initiative and Human Response in Ezekiel*. JSOT-Sup 51. Sheffield: JSOT Press.

———. 1996. Dislocation and Adaptation in the Exilic Age and After. In *After the Exile*, ed. J. Barton and D. J. Reimer, 45–58. Macon, GA: Mercer University Press.

Kutsko, J. F. 2000. *Between Heaven and Earth: Divine Presence and Absence in the Book of Ezekiel*. BJS 7. Winona Lake, IN: Eisenbrauns.

McKeating, H. 1993. *Ezekiel*. OTG. Sheffield: Sheffield Academic Press.

Mein, A. 2001. *Ezekiel and the Ethics of Exile*. Oxford Theological Monographs. Oxford: Oxford University Press.

Odell, M. S., and J. T. Strong, eds. 2000. *The Book of Ezekiel: Theological and Anthropological Perspectives*. SBLSymS 9. Atlanta: Society of Biblical Literature.

Raitt, T. M. 1977. *A Theology of Exile: Judgment/Deliverance in Jeremiah and Ezekiel*. Philadelphia: Fortress Press.

Schwartz, B. J. 2000. Ezekiel's Dim View of Israel's Restoration. In *The Book of Ezekiel*, ed. M. S. Odell and J. T. Strong, 43–67.

Wilson, R. R. 1972. Interpretation of Ezekiel's Dumbness. *VT* 22:91–104.

Zimmerli, W. 1965. The Special Form and Traditio-Historical Character of Ezekiel's Prophecy. *VT* 15:515–27.

———. 1979–83. *Ezekiel*. 2 vols. Hermeneia. Philadelphia: Fortress Press.

Jeremiah

Bright, J. 1965. *Jeremiah*. AB 21. 2nd ed., Garden City, NY: Doubleday.

Brueggemann, W. 1992. *Hopeful Imagination: Prophetic Voices in Exile*. Repr., London: SCM Press.

———. 1998. *A Commentary on Jeremiah: Exile and Homecoming*. Grand Rapids: Eerdmans.

Carroll, R. P. 1986. *Jeremiah: A Commentary*. OTL. London: SCM Press.

———. 2004. *Jeremiah*. T. & T. Study Guides. Repr., London: T. & T. Clark, Intl.

Clements, R. E. 1988. *Jeremiah*. Interpretation. Atlanta: John Knox Press.

Diamond, A. R. 1987. *The Confessions of Jeremiah in Context: Scenes in a Prophetic Drama*. JSOTSup 45. Sheffield: Sheffield Academic Press.

Holladay, W. L. 1989. *Jeremiah 2: A Commentary on the Book of the Prophet Jeremiah*, chaps. 26–52. Minneapolis: Fortress Press.

Janzen, J. G. 1973. *Studies in the Text of Jeremiah*. Cambridge: Cambridge University Press.

Leuchler, M. 2006. *Josiah's Reform and Jeremiah's Scroll: Historical Calamity and Prophetic Response*. Sheffield: Sheffield Pheonix Press.

McKane, W. 1986. *A Critical and Exegetical Commentary on Jeremiah*. Edinburgh: T. & T. Clark.

Mowinckel, S. 1946. *Prophecy and Tradition: The Prophetic Books in the Light of the Study of the Growth and History of the Tradition*. Kristiania: Jacob Dybwad.

Nicholson, E. W. 1970. *Preaching to the Exiles: A Study in the Prose Tradition in the Book of Jeremiah*. Oxford: Blackwell.

O'Connor, K. M. 1988. *The Confessions of Jeremiah: Their Interpretation and Role in Chapters 1–25*. Atlanta: Scholars Press.

———. 1989. "Do Not Trim a Word": The Contributions of Chapter 26 to the Book of Jeremiah. *CBQ* 51:617–30.

Raitt, T. M. 1977. *A Theology of Exile: Judgment/Deliverance in Jeremiah and Ezekiel*. Philadelphia: Fortress Press.

Seitz, C. R. 1985. The Crisis of Interpretation over the Meaning and Purpose of the Exile. *VT* 35:78–97.

———. 1989a. The Prophet Moses and the Canonical Shape of Jeremiah. *ZAW* 101:3–27.

———. 1989b. *Theology in Conflict: Reactions to the Exile in the Book of Jeremiah*. New York: de Gruyter.

Smith, M. S. 1990. *The Laments of Jeremiah and Their Contexts*. SBLMS 42. Atlanta: Scholars Press.

Stuhlman, L. 1986. *The Prose Sermons of the Book of Jeremiah: A Redescription of the Correspondences with the Detueronomistic Literature in the Light of Recent Text-critical Research*. SBLDS 83. Atlanta: Scholars Press.

———. 1998. *Order amid Chaos: Jeremiah as Symbolic Tapestry*. BS 57. Sheffield: Sheffield Academic Press.

Important Work in Languages Other than English

Duhm, B. 1901. *Das Buch Jeremia*. Tübingen: J. C. B. Mohr.

Mowinckel, S. 1914. *Zur Komposition des Buches Jeremia*. Kristiania: Jacob Dybwad.

Thiel, W. 1973. *Die Deuteronomistische Redaktion von Jeremia 1–25*, vol. 1. WMANT 41. Neukirchen-Vluyn: Neukirchener Verlag.

CHAPTER FIVE

General

Ackroyd, P. R. 1994. *Exile and Restoration*. Repr., London: XPress Reprints.

Albertz, R. 2003. *Israel in Exile: An Introduction to the History and Literature of the Sixth Century BCE*. Studies in Biblical Literature 3. Atlanta: SBL.

Brueggemann, W. 1992. *Hopeful Imagination: Prophetic Voices in Exile*. repr., London: SCM Press.

Lipschits, O. 2005. *The Fall and Rise of Jerusalem*. Winona Lake, IN: Eisenbrauns.

Deutero-Isaiah

Barstad, H. M. 1989. *A Way in the Wilderness. The "Second Exodus" in the Message of Second Isaiah*. JSSM 12. Manchester: University of Manchester.

———. 1997. *The Babylonian Captivity of the Book of Isaiah: "Exilic" Judah and the Provenance of Isaiah 40–55*. ISK. Oslo: Novus.

Blenkinsopp, J. 2002. *Isaiah 40–55*. AB 19A. New York: Doubleday.

Clements, R. E. 1982a. The Unity of the Book of Isaiah. *Int* 36:117–29.

Conrad, E. W. 1985. The Community as King in Second Isaiah. In *Understanding the Word*, ed. B. W. Anderson et al., 99–111. JSOTSup 36. Sheffield: JSOT Press.

Kapelrud, A. S. 1982. The Main Concern of Second Isaiah. *VT* 32:50–58.

Mettinger, T. N. D. 1983. *A Farewell to the Servant Songs*. Lund: Gleerup.

North, C. R. 1956. *The Suffering Servant in Deutero-Isaiah: An Historical and Critical Study*. 2nd ed., Oxford: Oxford University Press.

Sawyer, J. F. A. 1989. Daughter of Zion and Servant of the Lord in Isaiah: A Comparison. *JSOT* 44:89–107.

Westermann, C. 1969. *Isaiah 40–66*. OTL. London: SCM Press.

Whybray, R. N. 1975. *Isaiah 40–66*. NCB. London: Oliphants.

———. 1983. *The Second Isaiah*. OTG. Sheffield: JSOT Press.

Willey, P. T. 1995. The Servant of YHWH and Daughter Zion: Alternating Visions of YHWH's Community. *SBL 1995 Seminar Papers*: 267–303.

———. 1997. *Remember the Former Things: The Recollection of Previous Texts in Second Isaiah*. Atlanta, Scholars Press.

Williamson, H. G. M. 1994. *A Book Called Isaiah*. Oxford: Clarendon Press.

———. 1998. *Variations on a Theme: Kingship, Messiah, and Servant in the Book of Isaiah*, 113–66. Didsbury Lectures, 1997. Carlisle: Paternoster.

Ezekiel

Clements, R. E. 1982b. The Ezekiel Tradition: Prophecy in a Time of Crisis. In *Israel's Prophetic Tradition: Essays in Honour of Peter R. Ackroyd*, ed. R. Coggins, A. Phillips, and M. Knibb, 119–36. Cambridge: Cambridge University Press.

Greenberg, M. 1984. The Design and Themes of Ezekiel's Program of Restoration. *Int* 38:181–208.

Kutsko, J. F. 2000. *Between Heaven and Earth: Divine Presence and Absence in the Book of Ezekiel*. BJS 7. Winona Lake, IN: Eisenbrauns.

Levenson, J. D. 1976. *Theology of the Program of Restoration of Ezekiel 40–48*. Cambridge, MA: Harvard University Press.

Speiser, E. A. 1963. Background and Function of the Biblical NASI. *CBQ* 25:111–17.

CHAPTER SIX

General

Ackroyd, P. R. 1994. *Exile and Restoration*. Repr., London: XPress Reprints.

Alt, A. 1989. The Origins of Israelite Law. In *Essays on Old Testament History and Religion*. BS. Repr., Sheffield: JSOT Press.

Bedford, P. R. 2001. *Temple Restoration in Early Achaemenid Judah*. JSJSup 65. Leiden: Brill.

Childs, B. 1979. *Introduction to the Old Testament as Scripture*. Philadelphia: Fortress Press.

Driver, S. R. 1891. *An Introduction to the Literature of the Old Testament*. Edinburgh: T. & T. Clark. Although older, Driver provides many arguments for reasons to delineate the literature according to sources.

Hanson, P. D. 1975. *The Dawn of Apocalyptic*. Philadelphia: Fortress Press.

Lipschits, O. 2005. *The Fall and Rise of Jerusalem*. Winona Lake, IN: Eisenbrauns.

Mason, R. 1990. *Preaching the Tradition: Homily and Hermeneutics after the Exile*. Cambridge: Cambridge University Press.

McCarthy, D. J. 1978. *Treaty and Covenant: A Study in Form in the Ancient Oriental Documents and in the Old Testament*. Analecta Biblica 21A. Rome: Biblical Institute Press.

Nogalski, J. 1993. *Redactional Processes in the Book of the Twelve*. BZAW 218. Berlin: de Gruyter.

Orton, D. E., ed. 2000. *Prophecy in the Hebrew Bible: Selected Studies from Vetus Testamentum*. Brill's Readers in Biblical Studies 5. Leiden: Brill.

Rendtorff, R. 1986. *The Old Testament: An Introduction*. Philadelphia: Fortress Press.

Weinberg, J. 1992. *The Citizen–Temple Community*. JSOTSup 151. Sheffield: JSOT Press.

Haggai and Zechariah 1–8

Ackroyd, P. R. 1951. Studies in the Book of Haggai. *JJS* 2:163–76.

———. 1952. Studies in the Book of Haggai, Continued. *JJS* 3:151–56.

Clines, D. J. A. 1994. Haggai's Temple, Constructed, Deconstructed, and Reconstructed. In *Second Temple Studies*, vol. 2, *Temple Community in the Persian Period*, ed. T. C. Eskenazi and K. H. Richards, 60–87. JSOTSup 175. Sheffield: Sheffield Academic Press.

Hoffman, Y. 2003. The Fasts in the Book of Zechariah and the Fashioning of National Remembrance. In *Judah and the Judeans in the Neo-Babylonian Period*, ed. O. Lipschits and J. Blenkinsopp, 169–218. Winona Lake, IN: Eisenbrauns.

Mason, R. 1976. The Relation of Zechariah 9–14 to Proto-Zechariah. *ZAW* 88:227–39.

———. 1977. The Purpose of the Editorial Framework of the Book of Haggai. *VT* 27: 413–21.

Meyers, C. L., and E. M. Meyers. 1987. *Haggai, Zechariah 1–8*. AB 25B. New York: Doubleday.

Petersen, D. L. 1984. Zechariah's Visions: A Theological Perspective. *VT* 34:195–206.

Thomas, D. W. 1956. The Book of Haggai. In *The Interpreter's Bible*, 6:1037–49. Nashville: Abingdon Press.

Tollington, J. E. 1993. *Tradition and Innovation in Haggai and Zechariah 1–8*. JSOTSup 150. Sheffield: Sheffield Academic Press.

The Holiness Code and Leviticus

Auld, G. 2003. Leviticus between Exodus and Numbers. In *The Book of Leviticus*, ed. R. Rendtorff and R. A. Kugler, 41–54.

Clements, R. E. 1982. The Ezekiel Tradition: Prophecy in a Time of Crisis. In *Israel's Prophetic Tradition: Essays in Honour of Peter R. Ackroyd*, ed. R. Coggins, A. Phillips, and M. Knibb, 119–36. Cambridge: Cambridge University Press.

Douglas, M. 1999. *Leviticus as a Literature*. Oxford: Oxford University Press.

Gerstenberger, E. 1996. *Leviticus*. Old Testament Library. Louisville, KY: Westminster John Knox Press.

Joosten, J. 1996. *People and Land in the Holiness Code: An Exegetical Study of the Ideational Framework of the Law in Leviticus 17–26.* VTSup 67. Leiden: Brill.

Knohl, I. 1987. The Priestly Torah versus the Holiness School: Sabbath and Festivals. *HUCA* 58:65–117.

———. 1995. *The Sanctuary of Silence: The Priestly Torah and the Holiness School.* Minneapolis: Fortress Press.

Kratz, R. G. 2005. *The Composition of the Narrative Books of the Old Testament.* London: T. & T. Clark.

Levine, B. 2003. Leviticus: Its Literary History and Location in Biblical Literature. In *The Book of Leviticus,* ed. R. Rendtorff and R. A. Kugler, 11–23.

Milgrom, J. 1991. *Leviticus 1–16.* AB 3. New York: Doubleday.

———. 2000. *Leviticus 17–22.* AB 3a. New York: Doubleday.

———. 2001. *Leviticus 23–27.* AB 3b. New York: Doubleday.

Rendtorff, R., and R. A. Kugler, eds. 2003. *The Book of Leviticus: Composition and Reception.* VTSup 93 and FIOTL 3. Leiden: Brill.

Ross, A. P. 2002. *Holiness to the Lord: A Guide to the Exposition of the Book of Leviticus.* Grand Rapids: Baker Academic.

Sawyer, J., ed. 1996. *Reading Leviticus: A Conversation with Mary Douglas.* JSOTSup 227. Sheffield: Sheffield Academic Press.

Smith, C. R. 1996. The Literary Structure of Leviticus. *JSOT* 70:17–32.

Important Contributions in Languages Other than English

Beuken, W. A. M. 1967. *Haggai-Sacharja 1–8.* SSN 10. Assen: van Gorcum.

Petitjean, A. 1969. *Les Oracles du Proto-Zecharie: Un programme de restauration pour la communauté juive après l'exil.* Études Bibliques. Paris: Gabalda.

CONCLUSION

Boyarin, D., and J. Boyarin. 1993. Diaspora: Generation and the Ground of Jewish Identity. *Critical Inquiry* 19:693–725.

Brueggemann, W. 1997. *Cadences of Home: Preaching among Exiles.* Louisville, KY: Westminster John Knox Press.

Carroll, R. P. 1997. Deportation and Diasporic Discourses in the Prophetic Literature. In *Exile,* ed. J. Scott, 63–85.

Scott. J., ed. 1997. *Exile: Old Testament, Jewish, and Christian Conceptions.* Leiden: Brill.

Smith-Christopher, D. L. 2002. *A Biblical Theology of Exile.* Minneapolis: Fortress Press.

Scripture and Ancient Sources Index

Subject Index

Aaron, 64, 129
Adad-Guppi (mother of Nabonidus), 29
Ahab, 108
Ammon, 3, 16
Anathoth (village of), 67
Asdod, 11
Asherah, 21, 32
Ashkelon, 11
Assyrians, Assyrian Empire, Neo-Assyria, 10, 17, 23, 24, 30, 65, 67, 82

Baal, 28, 29, 32, 123
Babylonia, Babylonian empire, Neo-Babylon, ix, 1, 2, 3, 4, 5, 6, 7, 9, 10, 11, 12, 13, 14, 16, 17, 18, 19, 21, 22, 23, 24, 25, 26, 29, 30, 31, 33, 34, 35, 37, 38, 41, 45, 53, 55, 67, 69, 72, 73, 74, 76, 77, 78, 79, 82, 83, 84, 85, 86, 91, 93, 95, 96, 97, 98, 99, 100, 104, 105, 109, 113, 118, 120, 121, 124, 125, 126, 130, 135, 140, 141, 142, 143
Babylonian Exile, 24, 73, 77, 125, 134, 145, 149
Benjamin, region of, 13, 16, 30, 33, 53, 137
Beth Elohim , 30
Beth Yhwh (Yahweh), 18, 30, 31

Bethel, 18, 31, 33, 34, 54
Bethel-sharezer, 33

Cambyses, 13, 20
Carchemish, 10
communal dirge, 36, 37, 40, 50
communal laments, 29, 35, 36, 37, 38, 39, 40, 41, 42, 43, 44, 47, 50
covenant, 3, 27, 31, 32, 37, 39, 42, 43, 47, 48, 49, 50, 53, 56, 57, 61, 63, 66, 69, 71, 74, 78, 79, 84, 85, 89, 92, 93, 110, 113, 115, 118, 119, 125, 129, 130, 131, 132, 133, 134, 135, 138
creation, 63, 106, 107, 108, 109, 110, 125
   and election, 107, 109
   and history, 110
Cyrus, 2, 12, 13, 93, 95, 96, 97, 98, 99, 101, 109, 141
Cyrus Cylinder, 12, 13

Daniel, 85
Darius, 13, 116
David, Davidic, Davidide, 38, 39, 40, 45, 46, 50, 53, 54, 55, 56, 57, 59, 60, 62, 75, 76, 87, 110, 111, 116, 117, 120, 122
Davidic covenant, 39, 50, 56, 57, 59, 62, 66, 110